J

RALPH VAUGHAN WILLIAMS

Frontispiece photograph by Douglas Glass

RALPH VAUGHAN WILLIAMS, O.M.

Ralph
Vaughan Williams

A Discovery of his Music

by

SIMONA PAKENHAM

LONDON
MACMILLAN & CO LIMITED
NEW YORK · ST MARTIN'S PRESS
1957

MACMILLAN AND COMPANY LIMITED
London Bombay Calcutta Madras Melbourne

THE MACMILLAN COMPANY OF CANADA LIMITED
Toronto

ST MARTIN'S PRESS INC
New York

PRINTED IN GREAT BRITAIN

For

NOEL

CONTENTS

FRONTISPIECE

Ralph Vaughan Williams, O.M., from the photograph by Douglas Glass

vii

ACKNOWLEDGEMENTS

My THANKS are due to Novello and Co. Ltd, for permission to quote a passage from *A Short Account of Modern Music and Musicians* by W. McNaught; to George G. Harrap and Co. Ltd, for quotations from *Ralph Vaughan Williams: A Study* by Hubert Foss; to John Lane the Bodley Head for the quotation from Peter Warlock's *Delius* that stands at the head of my first chapter; and, above all, to Dr. R. Vaughan Williams, O.M. and the Oxford University Press for many quotations from *Some Thoughts on Beethoven's Choral Symphony* and for excerpts from programme notes and the notes attached to some of the musical scores.

On a more personal level I would like to thank three people but for whose moral support and exhortation this book would never have seen the light of day: my husband, Noel Iliff, for his alternate bullying and encouragement, and for his firmness and determination in despatching me in all weathers to concerts in remote and uncomfortable places; to Derek Hudson, the first professional writer to read this manuscript, for his insistence that it should not be thrown away and his subsequent advice as to what I ought to do with it; finally to Joseph Macleod, for sharing my enthusiasm for the subject of this book, and for his blue-pencilling of the manuscript, which was painful, salutary, and invariably right. None of these people made any comment whatsoever, much as they may have wanted to, on the opinions expressed in the book. For these I am alone responsible. They confined their criticism to advice on literary matters and matters of musical fact. To them I give my thanks, also to many of my friends who accompanied me, occasionally with deep misgivings, to concerts in out-of-the-way places, and sometimes rewarded me by coming away from them as enthusiastic as I was myself.

CHAPTER I

DISCOVERY

The average music lover does not approach music by the highroad of
history, still less by technical knowledge. His early experiences of
music are largely fortuitous. To him music is, as it were, a strange
element into which he is plunged from time to time. Then, one day,
he will experience something akin to an initiation. He will hear some
work to which his whole being seems to respond and from that day he
will cease to be content with such music as chance occasions may offer
him.

PETER WARLOCK

It happened to me as I was ironing at half-past eleven on a sunny
morning in 1942. I had switched on the wireless as an accompaniment to my labours, a habit I deplored in other people but
practised in private myself — quietly! The schools programmes
were my favourite entertainment in those days, as indeed they are
still, and I timed such chores as the ironing to coincide with them
in the hope of absorbing a little of the education which had passed
over my head at school and which, no doubt, was passing even at
that moment over the heads of countless children for whom it was
intended. That morning, however many heads it may have passed
over, it did not pass over mine. It took a lower aim and struck me
a stunning blow in whatever region lies the seat of the affections,
a blow from which, more than a decade later, I am dizzy still.
Music assaulted and transported me; music I did not understand
but which, instead of forbidding by its strangeness, filled me with
a desperate longing for more and more; music which, for all its
unfamiliarity, had a puzzling and elusive echo as if of something
I had forgotten but had once known intimately. I waited, trembl-
ing, for enlightenment. I fixed my eyes upon that commonplace
object, my wireless, with a new and wondering respect. I think
and hope that I turned off the iron.

The voice within my radio informed the schools and me that this was music by an Englishman. Imagine, if you can, the effect of such a statement on my unprepared ears! This, as I have said, was 1942. I hope it could not happen now, for musical education has advanced by leaps and bounds during the last few years. My own musical education had been scandalously lacking, but one thing at least had been firmly fixed in my head — that my countrymen suffered from the disability of being unable either to produce or adequately to comprehend musical sounds. So all my illusions were abruptly shattered. I heard, coming through my loudspeaker, not only music by an Englishman, but music with intense individuality and aggressive power; music that sounded to my unskilled ears quite unlike anything produced by the reputedly musical nations, and perfectly able to compete on its own merits with anything they had produced. The music was part of a Symphony in F minor. The composer's name — Vaughan Williams.

This is the history of an obsession, I had better confess that at the outset, to make my position clear — in case any intending reader may be deceived into thinking that this is a scholarly book about music. It is something quite different. It is the shocking personal revelations of a secret music addict and consequently quite unfit for publication.

A music addict, however, as anybody who knows one will tell you, is the fiercest of all propagandists. Reserving the right to withdraw from the world from time to time and shut ourselves away with our favourite works, we direct the rest of our energies to the conversion of our friends to whatever musical work, composer, or group of composers happen to be obsessing us at the moment. Two separate and violently antagonistic forces are constantly at work within us; the one urging us to go upon the roof-tops and thence exhort the populace to listen to our beloved composers in order that, if they happen to be living ones, they may be 'honoured in their generation' and become 'the glory of their times'; the opposing force holding us back, whispering unworthily that it is intolerable that they should become popular, that some work that has ravished us should be handed on to others whose sensibilities are not nearly as exquisite as we imagine our own to be. These contradictory urges battle within us to our dying day. There is no hope whatever of their reconciliation. Fortunately sanity and — is it really as bad as that? — a desire to have our own opinions endorsed by the world at large, win in the end, and we become confirmed propagandists.

If a professional musician, therefore, should chance to open this book and read these words I hope that he will behave as honour-ably as he would like to imagine himself behaving if he came upon a bundle of somebody else's letters to his wife. For, clearly, this is not the book for him. On page 194 a list is waiting, ready to guide him to literature on this subject that is more fitted to his status in the world. This is a book for the ordinary listener; the listener, like myself, whose world, because we live in the twentieth century, has been invaded, by way of the radio and the long-playing record, by an art which might, in another age, have passed us by com-pletely; for the listener wanting to know more about music who ir, as yet, a little intimidated by learned books full of musical quotations that need a trained ear or a conveniently situated piano before their relevance to the text can be appreciated. But before going on to the subject of this history I feel it is necessary to sketch in a little of the background against which my own adven-ture took place, if only to make it clear how momentous for me the incident of that sunny summer morning really was; how the chance hearing of a few bars of music set me off on a journey of exploration and discovery that was to last for many years.

The generation I was born in went to school between two wars. We had the twenties of our lives virtually stolen from us by the second of them. But our musical troubles had their origin much further back than that. They began when our parents, exhausted by an earlier and, in some ways, grimmer war, determined at all costs that no suffering of the kind they had endured in their own youth should be inflicted on their own helpless children. So thay conferred upon us the blessings jazz had brought them. They filled our ears from birth with tunes played scratchily upon that marvellous invention — the gramophone — with its alarming menacing horn. By the time we reached school the wireless was a common-place. I cannot remember that it played anything but dance music.

It is a well-known medical fact that too much isolation can be dangerous. If you try to insure that your children never meet a germ you render them far more liable to succumb when, inevit-ably, in later life, germs come their way. Their constitution has had no chance to build its antibodies ready to fight in the daily encounter with a host of microbes. To shut your children away from music can be just as dangerous. For my generation, kept practically in ignorance that such an art existed, music became a deadly peril. There were, of course, the fortunate minority who could not fall victim to its ravages — the tone-deaf, and the mem-bers of the musical profession, which somehow always manages to find recruits to enable it to survive. Nobody who can extract any tune they desire from a violin; who can sit down to a piano and conjure from its inscrutable black and white keys the work of any composer in the world; or who can open a score and receive from it anything better than a sense of frustration or complete impotence, has any real idea of what we others suffer. They have been inoculated against the disorder by the vigorous practice of scales in early youth, by a conscientious eye trained upon the tip of the conductor's baton, by initiation into the mysteries of har-mony and counterpoint.

In the sixteenth century, when the lute in the barber's shop dis-charged the function fulfilled now by *Picture Post*, and the man who could not read a part at sight in the after-dinner madrigal was deeply and properly ashamed, there can have been no ques-tion of such a state of affairs. There was no cinema in those days for parents to pack their children off to, so, conscientiously, they saw to it that they carried about with them the means to woo their young ladies and work off their moods of melancholy. Poor subjects they would have been for psycho-analysis.

The Victorian era was another matter; but nobody, especially no young person, failed to become inoculated when persistently requested to 'bring their music' to an evening party, and who, suitably dressed in virgin white, sang her sad little song or played her Chopin Prelude on the upright piano or, relegated to a position of less importance but infinitely greater responsibility, accompanied her handsome uncle in some dashing or heartrending ballad. Our parents were put through similar embarrassments a generation later. They practised their Czerny, and were sometimes rewarded with a luscious piece of Liszt, sitting with straight backs and dangling feet before the inevitable upright, endeavouring to accompany the relentless metronome or the 'one and two and three and — ' of the no less relentless music mistress. It is understandable that they reacted. They determined to be better parents themselves; to refrain from subjecting their own young to the horror of music lessons — the ruler poised ready to rap knuckles not bent to the precise degree; studies; scales; five-finger exercises and arpeggios; the dreary and monotonous labour that led no higher than the 'Maiden's Prayer' or being allowed to accompany at school hymn-singing. I suppose it was not their fault that they brought us up with one sense missing; one avenue of self-expression closed to us. They believed themselves wise, economical and kind; they thought they were preserving our souls as well as our knuckles. The extra in our school bills was no longer 'music', it was 'domestic economy'. In place of 'fancy needlework, watercolour painting and pianoforte' we had 'dressmaking, cookery and book-keeping'.

Of course, if any of us showed unmistakable signs of musical genius, and could not be deterred from strumming on the few pianos as yet unsold or covering sheets of music-paper with illegible fugues they tackled the situation with bravery, resignation and good sense. After consultation with the doctor, the school teacher and the Bank manager they procured the best instructors available and allowed the musical talent scope for growth, praying all the time that it might in the end prove an illusion. So a generation and a half were turned out of people sharply divided into two classes — one very small, the other comprising almost all of us — the musician and the person with no music at all. The amateur practically vanished. The unlucky ones with insufficient talent to make music a paying proposition, or who simply had no idea that music existed except as a mysterious rite for a small and remote clique, entertained themselves at the cinema, wooed their young ladies to the strains of all the dance bands broadcast by the B.B.C., and worked off their moods of melancholy, according to temperament, with a game of tennis or the poems of Rupert Brooke.

Our schools tackled the problem in their own peculiar way. At the end of term there would be a concert. This was a function at which those superior pupils who got themselves labelled 'musical' showed off their prowess to the bored unmusical majority, the warmth of whose applause was more a testimony to the popularity of the performer than the excellence of the performance. The musical pupils deserved their brief moment of glory as a recompence for the opprobrium that had descended on their heads, for, when all right-minded people were going out to games, they could be seen vanishing furtively with their music-cases towards the practice cubicles. If the applause was sometimes a little thin it was partly a result of the inadequate sound-proofing of the practice rooms that had somewhat staled the novelty of the 'Moonlight' Sonata which had been diligently 'got up' for the occasion during the previous three months.

Then there was 'Musical Appreciation' — half an hour a week for everybody, tone-deaf or musical alike. At any school equipped with a radiogram the formula on alternate Saturdays was this: 'Now shut your eyes and listen, and then write down the sort of picture the music suggests to you.' This was boring for the tone-deaf; for the musical it must have been sheer torture; but for the half-and-betweens who made up the majority in any school it was the greatest fun of the week. It was fun, that is to say, when we heard 'The Carnival of the Animals', or 'The Sorcerer's Apprentice', or the 'New World' Symphony; but a bore when it was the turn of Bach or Mozart or even Mendelssohn's 'Dream'. On the other Saturdays we begged in vain for the radiogram. They set us other tasks. Laboriously we learned to draw our leger lines, to decorate them accurately with the curliest of treble clefs, the most streamlined of bass ones. We copied crotchets and minims, triplets and semiquavers, appoggiaturas (whatever they may be) and various types of rest. We could spell and understand all the Italian musical terms. We knew all there was to know about written music except what it ought to sound like. We had all left school before reaching that part of the lesson. Half an hour on alternate Saturdays can turn out few composers.

There was at least one aspect of school music-making that was effectively encouraged, and enjoyed — singing, especially choir practice. Between the wars our singing classes fell heirs to the gleanings of the folk-song collectors, and the songs were good to sing. A few modern part-songs came our way, though it was only in later years that some of us discovered they were modern; a renewed interest was beginning to be taken in the music of the forgotten polyphonists. For all we knew Byrd and John Ireland were contemporaries, but we enjoyed singing songs by both of them. *Hymns A & M* was superseded by the robuster *Songs of Praise*. Singing classes supplied for our brief school-days something remotely akin to the music-making of the sixteenth century. When we left school we felt their loss more deeply than any other. They had provided us with the one vital musical experience of our lives.

In the world that awaited the young person emerging self-consciously from the protective chrysalis that school afforded there seemed to be no place for that sort of thing. We could not sing 'Jerusalem' in our baths. It demands the full-voiced enthusiasm of a large crowd of people; besides our mothers would exclaim 'What a depressing noise!' and turn on the radio to drown us. In church we discovered that grown-ups did not sing and embarrassment forced us also to be silent throughout our favourite hymns. At home we were astonished to hear our most cherished of 'Musical Appreciation' pieces condemned as dreary, if we happened to come upon one when knob-twiddling and dared to listen for a moment. We had some sympathy with our elders for being unable to abide Bach, but it was hard to understand their condemnation of Dvořák, Borodin and Tchaikovsky as well, all

B R.V.W.

under the general heading of 'classical music'. We were out in the world at last; we were under the illusion that we were educated, for our teachers had omitted to tell us that education is a voluntary process for which school is a mere preparation. We were anxious to behave like grown-up people in a grown-up world. What model should we follow but our parents? So we went to the cinema, we accepted every invitation to dance that came our way, and, as if that were not enough, we allowed the B.B.C. to fill our homes with dance music at all hours of the day and night.

Some of us came into contact with people of our grand-parents' generation who, for the most part, had not become jazz-fans and were inclined to protest if we made night hideous with the radio in their houses. They had not quite grown accustomed to this invention of the devil and consequently used it with more intelligent discrimination than we who had. It was they who took us to an occasional concert, plunging us 'from time to time' into that 'strange element', music. From them we learnt that there existed *three* kinds of music, not merely two as we had previously believed. We knew already of the great gulf fixed between 'classical music' and 'dance music'. Now we discovered that there existed a third kind, divided from the others by a gulf infinitely greater — 'modern music'. This was spoken of in hushed tones, and, as it did not appear in the concerts to which we were taken, we remained ignorant of its nature and horribly awed by its very name.

This was the background to my generation. This was the vulnerable condition in which we were loosed upon the world, some of us with the uncomfortable inkling that we were missing something vital not only to our happiness but to our very lives. What happened to us? Well, there were the ones who saw to it that their supply of jazz and swing never ran short, by singing it aloud or shoving on a record, when, by some unfortunate omission, the B.B.C. had none to offer. They were quite safe, unable even to be conscious of the pangs of unfulfilled desire so long as they were able to maintain this protective envelope of sound. Some of us discovered the Proms. Those whose constitutions were strong enough managed to keep their feet night after night throughout the two months' ordeal, absorbing whatever was on the menu however exotic, however homely. Then they, to all appearance, dismissed the art of music from their lives from the last hysterical Prom in September to the first rapturous Prom of the following July. Others of us reacted, as the young will surely do, against our parents' boredom with the classics and our grandparents' horror of the moderns. One large group of people was sent scurrying back to Bach, score in hand and spectacles on nose; and another precipitated violently towards Stravinsky and 'Les Six', who, though we did not know it, were only our grandparents' idea of 'modern' and were busily becoming dated all the time; for 'modern' still seems to mean to the average person the music of the 1920's and somebody will have to coin a new title to cover the music of our times. The reactions of both these groups were largely artificial, for they listened to music earnestly and in protest, a certain way of preventing music creeping in beneath the skin.

We must not forget the Balletomane, most fascinating of phenomena. Few of us escaped the rabid germs of Balletomania, which caught our elders too, with very odd effect. It reconciled them, most improbably, for the brief space of their sojourn in the theatre, to the most academic of the classics and the most cacophonous of the moderns, though it did not in the least effect their attitude to the same noises when heard outside, unaccompanied by dancing. We were dazzled by the lights, the colours, the coruscating ballerinas, by the personalities of the Massines, Woizikowskys and Helpmanns, and did not understand that it was the music that had really taken hold of our imagination, the music that supplied at least half the light, the colour, the personality.

In these various ways my contemporaries approached the world of music, sometimes furtively, for fear of ridicule, sometimes defiantly, almost always hiding a secret inferiority complex because so few of us could play an instrument or even remember the simple four-part harmony that most of us had managed roughly to decipher at school prayers. The world of music appeared closed

to us and none of us had the confidence to pronounce aloud our
personal judgement on a single composer or musical work unless
it had been backed by at least a century of critical approbation.
We were waiting, though we did not know it, for a revelation.

Let me quote again the passage by Peter Warlock, from his
book about his favourite composer, Delius, that stands at the beginning of this chapter, for I am sure no truer word was ever
written about the shattering process of musical awakening that a
chance hearing may bring to a person living peacefully with never
a thought that music had any meaning in their life.

'The average music lover does not approach music by the highroad of history, still less by technical knowledge. His early experiences of music are largely fortuitous. To him music is, as it were,
a strange element into which he is plunged from time to time.
Then, one day, he will experience something akin to an initiation. He will hear some work to which his whole being seems
to respond and from that day he will cease to be content with such
music as chance occasions may offer him.'

That was precisely what happened to me when I switched on
my wireless and heard part of a Symphony in F minor by Ralph
Vaughan Williams.

Anybody who has experienced the initiation Peter Warlock
spoke of will understand my reactions very well, whether the
initiation was by way of Bach, or Delius, the subject of Warlock's
essay; possibly by Warlock's own music; or some chance song,
like 'Agincourt', fresh and shining out of the shadows of antiquity.
We have encountered the one kind of music to which our whole
being can respond, which sets chords vibrating in our memory
that never responded to the best music of the greatest masters. A
sense of recognition always dominates this upheaval — and an
upheaval it certainly is — subconsciously we have always known
this music existed. We have been waiting for it, though we did
not know it, all our lives. We have heard nothing like it, and yet
it is not strange at all. From that day onwards music is no longer a
strange element for us to be plunged in from time to time. Diving

in headlong we are astonished to find, at last, that we can swim.
We cease, as Warlock predicted, to be content with the music
chance occasions have to offer. We become autocratic, choosy,
and are caught slinking off to concerts all alone.

We ordinary listeners, after suffering this sudden immersion,
find curious things happening to us. We discover that music,
though primarily still something to be listened to, is also something to be read about, and thought about, and dreamed about.
We comb the shelves of the Public Library for every volume that
will throw a glimmer of light on our new-found delight. Inexpert
as we are, we find a score reveals utterly unsuspected glories in our
too familiar gramophone records. We retire into a corner and
think about music, or go for long walks in the country and, taking
no notice of the birds, the trees, the clouds above our heads, concentrate all our mind and all our senses on the memory of some
work we have recently heard. Indulged in built-up areas this habit
no doubt adds to the horrifying total of road accidents, for it is
not only the pedestrian who can be so afflicted. Such a visitation
may come upon us as we ride our bicycle or drive our car. It
would be well for the unmusical to bear this in mind; the harm-
less-looking cyclist approaching down the road may be absorbed
in the ninth movement of Messiaen's 'Turangalîla' Symphonie,
and what might not happen then?

We, who are not trained musicians, cannot reproduce in our
heads, try as we may, the complete sounds of an orchestra; we
have no conception of the blessed condition of being a composer
and able to carry one around in one's head. We ponder on the
essence of the music, rather than its details. We seek to discover how
certain sequences of notes are able to produce such violent reactions in ourselves; we try to penetrate further into the mysterious
country whose frontiers we have so recently crossed. We behave
exactly like the lover of tradition, and the world is transformed
for us as for him. We walk unseeing, our senses all turned inward
in contemplation of our latest musical experience; the *Radio Times*
is opened with trepidation for fear of what it may reveal; we blush
at the sight of Saturday's *Daily Telegraph*; we beg the newsagent

for the Prom list weeks before its publication is due; we catch ourselves hastily switching off the wireless at the sound of an approaching footstep in case we might be caught in unholy indulgence in
Monteverdi or Schoenberg or whoever our particular obsession
may be; we tread on air and are possessed of new eyes, going
about our daily occupations observing the smallest details as buildings and trees alike revolve in a stately Sarabande, or shout aloud
for joy with all the Sons of God.

It was all very well for Peter Warlock when he found himself
bowled over and suffered a shocking derangement and reversal of
all his preconceived ideas on first hearing the music of his beloved
Delius. He was already a musician. There were things he could do
to alleviate his condition. He could pick up a Delius score and read
it as we read a book, familiarising himself at will with the delicious
new music, not having to wait for years, as we might, to track it
down to a concert performance. He could go on composing,
allowing his new-found source of inspiration to work through
him and give his music wings. He did not have to go and shout
upon the roof-tops of his enthusiasm and his joy; he was able,
instead, to write a scholarly and erudite book on the composer
who meant so much to him, a book that could sit confidently on
the shelves beside the writings of any musician in the world.

What a case am I in then, who can neither compose nor get
much pleasure from a printed score unless it be of music that I
know a little, that I dare to comment on the writings of such a
composer as Vaughan Williams! Yet my need, my instinct to go
upon the roof-tops and shout aloud is every bit as compelling as
Warlock's was.

So I write the following chapters — not a scholarly and erudite
book, but a shouting on the roof-tops to anybody who will listen
— for three reasons. To try to discover for myself why the notes
put together by this one particular composer should produce in
me effects that no other music can parallel. The composer in
question, in a comforting article on score reading, 'The Letter
and the Spirit', wrote this (my favourite definition of what
music is) — 'What the musical composer, in effect, says to

his performers is; "I desire to produce a certain spiritual result on certain people. I hope and believe that if you blow, and scrape, and hit in a particular manner this spiritual effect will result." ' Of course I cannot be certain that the 'spiritual effect' made upon me by the thousands of musicians I must have heard since 1942 devotedly blowing and scraping and hitting the notes Vaughan Williams put down on paper, is the precise 'spiritual effect' he desired to produce; but he could hardly have hoped for anything more overwhelming. In those years that music has given me more pleasure than the work of any artist in any medium whatsoever, and the pleasure continues to grow and deepen with every new work, with each successive hearing of the old ones. So my second reason for writing is as a small inadequate thanksgiving for all the joy received; my third, a passionate and tub-thumping desire that as many people as I can persuade — ordinary concert-goers like myself — may share in my delight.

CHAPTER II

EXPLORATION

Ralph Vaughan Williams is a composer who walks in heaven. Not perhaps, like Bach, at all times, hardly noticing that he does so; nor is heaven revealed to him in a sudden blaze of glory as, they say, it was to Handel. The key is in his pocket and he ascends there for his refreshment and ours when he is tired of wandering the lowlands of the English countryside, or exhausted by his frequent battles with the powers of darkness. Of the three levels of creation exemplified on the stage in his ballet 'Job' and Blake's drawings, from which part of its inspiration was drawn, the heavenly level seems, at any rate in his old age, to be the one on which he is most at home. He can throw wide heaven's gates to us in the stately Sarabande and Galliard from that ballet; he can draw us up with him in joy with the stirring 'Te Deum' he wrote for the Coronation of 1937. It needs but little effort on our part to enjoy these broad and simple tunes; but sometimes he sets out upon a journey into a region that is alien to our minds and ears and, if we would follow him there, we must first strengthen ourselves to accept the uncompromising directness of his vision, and come, also, to terms with the ruthless attitude he takes towards conventional harmony.

It is unlikely that in 1956 anybody can be as shockingly ignorant of Vaughan Williams's existence and stature as I was in 1942. However deaf one had remained to his music one could hardly fail to be aware of the celebrations later in the same year and again in 1952 that marked his seventieth and eightieth birthdays. Even those, however, who, like me, discovered his music when he was nearly seventy have probably been singing it for years. Most people know his tune 'Sine Nomine' for the hymn 'For all the

Saints' — a magnificent march which, by itself, could have in-
sured his immortality; and many are on intimate terms with the
lovely gentle music of his Whitsun hymn 'Come Down, O Love
Divine'. He called this tune 'Down Ampney' after the Gloucestershire village where his father was vicar and where, in 1872, he was
born.

My school, in the 1930's, used to look forward to Empire Day,
because we enjoyed the songs that were appropriate to that otherwise depressing festival better than any others we had to sing in
the whole year. I can remember only one to which we attached a
composer — 'Land of Hope and Glory'. We were vaguely aware
of Elgar. It was not that his existence made any difference to our
views about the total lack of English music — in a land without
composers here was a great composer; the exception to prove the
rule. We got no further in our study of his music than this one
plush-upholstered tune. We were utterly incurious as to who had
written the other tunes for that day's celebrations — 'Jerusalem',
'I Vow to Thee, my Country' and 'Let us now Praise Famous
Men', three rousing good songs unencumbered, so far as we knew
or cared, with composers. The last of these was my own favourite
and, if I ever noticed the name R. Vaughan Williams on the top
right-hand corner of the sheet of music, I never remembered it
long enough to connect it with the name which, I imagine,
appeared in *Songs of Praise* above the tunes 'Sine Nomine' and
'Down Ampney'.

The discovery that these three tunes, which I had regarded as
part of my ancient heritage, were in fact the work of the very
composer whose Symphony in F minor had bowled me over,
was a revelation almost as startling as the incident of the ironing-
board had been to me, and even more illuminating. It would
be fanciful to try to pretend that these three hymns which I had
known so long did anything to prepare my ears for that symphony; but in the flowing shapeliness of the Whitsun hymn, and
the plain ecstatic vigour of the other tunes, lie the germs of much
that is characteristic in Vaughan Williams's style.

Vaughan Williams was a late developer. If he had died at

Mozart's age he would have left a name no greater than his contemporary and friend George Butterworth left, and a list of works hardly as long. His career has been a steady progress towards technical mastery, always a little outstripped by his imaginative power, for he has never found composing easy, until, at over eighty, he is turning out not only his most ambitious and perfected works, but appears to be turning them out in larger numbers. His output has steadily risen over the years with only one bare patch in the list of his achievements coinciding with the 1914 war. There remain very few works dating from before his late thirties that he has not withdrawn. He was approaching sixty when he began to write the sort of music that staggered the critics and shocked the public by its modernity. The slow crescendo of achievement, shown by the complete list of his works, seems to have the inevitability of a great organic growth, as if there had been no halting or hesitating, no anxious self-examination, no doubts at all. This impression is entirely misleading.

It was while I was still lost in admiration of the last two new works by Vaughan Williams that I had been fortunate enough to hear — the immense 'Sinfonia Antartica' with its vast orchestra in which every instrument has a distinctive and unreplaceable part, and the mellow, beautifully scored 'Oxford Elegy', that I came, by chance, on the following little passage in a book by Gwen Raverat: 'An amusing recollection of this very young age — ' she tells us, 'is of hearing scraps of conversation about "that foolish young man, Ralph Vaughan Williams", who *would* go on working at music when "he was so hopelessly bad at it." This memory is confirmed by a letter of Aunt Etty's: "He has been playing all his life, and for six months *hard*, and yet he can't play the smallest thing decently. They say it will simply break his heart if he is told that he is too bad to hope to make anything of it." '

In his short autobiography, written for the book *Ralph Vaughan Williams* by Hubert Foss, the composer confesses to the unusual difficulties that beset his way while he was trying to arrive at a musical idiom that would express his own personal vision. He studied under a great many distinguished teachers and has con-

tinued to seek for means of self-improvement from his first composition 'The Robin's Nest', a piece some four bars long which he
wrote when six years old, to his latest symphony which, almost
certainly, as is his habit, he'will'have submitted for criticism to many
musicians younger and less experienced than himself, before being
satisfied that it was ready for performance. His teachers included
Parry, Charles Wood, Stanford, Max Bruch and, finally, Maurice
Ravel, a man younger than himself, to whom he went at the age
of thirty-six because he had come to the conclusion that he was
'lumpy and stodgy, and had come to a dead end and that a little
French polish' would be of use to him. Yet during this rigorous
training he clung obstinately to his belief that certain shocking
errors that he loved to perpetrate and which sorely vexed his
learned masters were, in fact, fundamental to him. He must have
been an infuriating pupil! He felt in his bones that he was right
and the text-books on harmony wrong, and, when he discovered
English folk-song with that sense of recognition that accompanies
all great discoveries — ('here's something' he said 'which I have
known all my life — only I didn't know it') — he found himself
vindicated, and the shocking errors not only became basic to his
own style, but can be detected now in the music of many a
modern composer who does not even recognise Vaughan
Williams's influence.

No other composer seems to have waged so long a war to perfect his art, or perhaps it is only that no other composer has been
so frank about his difficulties or so ready with his tributes to those
who helped or influenced him, whether they were his teachers,
his fellow students, or even his own pupils: but he goes a little far,
surely, when, in the same autobiographical chapter, he utters the
pathetic cry — 'I have struggled all my life to conquer amateurish
technique, and, now that perhaps I have mastered it, it seems too
late to make use of it.' Since that sentence was written, in 1950,
the list of his works before me shows 'The Pilgrim's Progress', the
'Sinfonia Antartica', the Christmas Cantata 'Hodie' and the Symphony in D minor — to mention only those of his many works
that last over thirty minutes. Besides these large works there is also

chamber music, film and radio scores, a small concerto or two, his contributions to the coronation service, and various songs. I do not think that we need to pity him overmuch. There is very little outward evidence of amateurish technique in anything he has written since (to put it as late as possible) 'Job' in 1930, and this very amateurishness, if we are to accept his word that it exists, is partly responsible for the most exciting and the most revealing moments in his music. Lacking fluency, he has had to fight every inch of the way to capture the precise form to clothe his inspiration. Notes have never run trippingly off his pen and, very often, it is when the struggle for expression is most apparent that this music is at its most impressive. 'I don't know whether I like it, but it is what I meant,' he said, half apologetically, but half, I suspect, in triumph, after the F minor Symphony had blasted everybody's unprepared ears. In that case the meaning he was fighting to capture in orchestral sound dictated to his mind a new kind of music only hinted at before in the Satan episodes in 'Job'.

If I were a trained musician writing a cold and scholarly survey of Vaughan Williams's musical works this is the point at which you would expect to find some sort of general analysis of his style. But even if I were fitted to discharge so difficult a duty I am not sure I would want to do so. It is my hope that, as we pass by his works in roughly chronological order — roughly is as near as he and the various and contradictory reference books will allow us to get — we will see how that style was hammered out and developed in a way that description divorced from the works would never make clear. There are, however, one or two matters that need a brief examination before we pass on to these works. And I must begin with an apology.

Dr Vaughan Williams has not confined his writings to that which can be set in black and white upon the five-line staves of music-paper. I have already quoted from the brief musical autobiography in which he tells the story of the main influences, enthusiasms and prejudices that contributed to the making of his style. Most of his writings are to be found within the covers of two thinnish books — *National Music* and *Some Thoughts on Beet-*

hoven's Choral Symphony; the first a series of lectures delivered at Bryn Mawr College, Pennsylvania; the second a collection of miscellaneous essays on musical subjects. These essays, though only one of them is in any sense concerned with his own music, contain the answers to many of the questions that have been voiced by critics of his works over the long years that he has been composing, and, although it is, of course, strictly speaking, unnecessary to supplement our knowledge of his music by a reading of his opinions, yet, as we are human, we cannot fail to be helped and enlightened by these writings.

But to my apology. Vaughan Williams, in his analysis of Beethoven's Ninth Symphony, draws attention to the fact that he had read the analysis of that same work by Sir Donald Tovey, 'from which', he says, 'I must confess I have helped myself liberally.' In his *Musical Autobiography* he sets forth his views upon the art of 'cribbing'. 'Cribbing is, to my mind, a legitimate and praiseworthy practice, but one ought to know where one has cribbed.' And later in the same essay — 'I have never had any conscience about cribbing.' My own conscience is, I am afraid, a little tenderer than Vaughan Williams's, but I propose, throughout the succeeding pages, to accord him the 'sincerest flattery' of 'imitation' by helping myself liberally to such quotations from his writings as will illuminate them. As for cribbing — in my fourteen years' pursuit of his music I have read and re-read every single word on or by him that I could lay my hands on. I am generally aware when and from whom I have cribbed, but it is not always possible to make precise acknowledgements where many critics think alike. I can only beg indulgence and declare my profound indebtedness to the many writers who have helped me to a fuller understanding and, consequently, a more thorough enjoyment of my favourite music.

So let me help myself at once to a paragraph from Vaughan Williams's second book. It is one that should, in truth, stand over every page of this book, and of most books about music, as well. 'I know full well that music has no meaning in the material sense, and cannot be explained in terms of earthly fact. But, like all writers on music, I find it a convenient way, occasionally, of putting into words the scheme of the music.'

We also know full well that music has no material meaning. We have learned, if we have read any books about music at all, to frown on the descriptive; we have been bullied into the unquestioning acceptance that the purer and less programmatic a piece of music can be the worthier it is. Vaughan Williams sets us a problem. While agreeing verbally with this general opinion, he confuses us at the outset of our acquaintance with his compositions by seeming to attach a 'material' meaning to the vast majority of them. To the first three of his Symphonies he gave descriptive titles — the 'Sea', the 'London', the 'Pastoral'; for the next three he abandoned this practice, calling them, more austerely, F minor, D major, E minor. Yet, in the case of the D major Symphony he appended a quotation from *The Pilgrim's Progress* to one of the movements, and, though he removed it before the score was published, he left us in no doubt that in that book lay the source of his inspiration. Finally in the 'Sinfonia Antartica' he shamelessly offered us a colossal piece of programme music, one that would lose half its greatness if the audience did not know something of the story that inspired it. It is unnecessary to know the titles 'London' or 'Pastoral' to enjoy the music of those symphonies (the 'Sea' Symphony, since it is choral, is a different matter), but the 'Antartica' would be puzzling indeed to a listener totally unaware of its scenario.

Setting aside the operas, ballets and choral music in which the source of the inspiration is plain for all to read, only the concertos — violin, piano, oboe and bass tuba — the unnamed symphonies, and the two string quartets have no 'material' connections. A list of the titles of his lesser works might suggest Vaughan Williams was indeed a composer of descriptive music — the 'Norfolk' Rhapsodies; 'In the Fen Country'; 'The Lark Ascending'; 'On Christmas Night'. His 'Five Variants of Dives and Lazarus'; the 'Household Music', based on Welsh hymn tunes; and his most famous work of all, the great 'Fantasia on a Theme by Thomas Tallis', come to one's ears not only as meditations on the music they examine but also, it seems, on the whole period and way of life that gave that music birth. Even 'Flos Campi', the most enig. matic music he ever wrote, is decorated all over with verses from the 'Song of Songs'. Yet there is little pictorial detail — the 'London' Symphony with its chiming clock and strident road-side band holds almost the sum total — though the 'Sinfonia Antartica', which is an exception to all the rules, shows Vaughan Williams to be as good a writer of descriptive music as anybody would wish to be. The 'Pastoral' Symphony has no description in it: it is a work of distilled contemplation, abstract and pure as Bach. In this score you will find no Delius cuckoos, no Beethoven quails, not even his own lark ascending. 'Vaughan Williams', wrote one critic, 'lets us forget everything except that there is music going on.' Under the surface of this music the thought runs slow and deep, questioning and wondering, breaking in places through the soft landscape of orchestral colour like rugged roots and stones.

Perversely (and 'perversely' is a word that is likely to appear upon these pages again and again) it is the unnamed symphonies that seem to carry the most urgent weight of 'meaning', although, certainly, they cannot be explained 'in terms of earthly fact'. It was the F minor Symphony, followed by the serene D major, that earned Vaughan Williams his reputation as a prophet; the one, said the critics, foreshadowing war; the other, first performed in war, prophesying peace. In these unnamed symphonies the weight of thought, philosophy and contemplation is overwhelming. Only Beethoven writes music with this moral force — Beethoven, whose style repels Vaughan Williams, whose mind fascinates him, and with whose symphonies his own have sometimes been compared. It is as much the message that each symphony carries as the different style in which each is written that makes it impossible, after even a brief acquaintance, to confuse a movement of any one of them with a movement of any other, for the style and the message are one.

If a listener sets out, as I did, upon an exploration to discover all his music — in concert lists, in gramophone catalogues and in the

Radio Times — and patiently listen to it all, it is the astonishing variety of his styles that will probably strike him first, and not only in the symphonies. At first it is not easy to hear anything in common between, for instance, 'The Wasps' Overture, the song-cycle, 'On Wenlock Edge', and the 'Fantasia on a Theme by Thomas Tallis', to take three works performed within two years. The subject-matter dictates the form and style, each new work presenting the composer with a separate problem so that, in his unsparing search for the exact truth, he has had to forge himself each time new tools with which to solve it.

It is difficult for a listener of a later generation than Vaughan Williams's own to appreciate exactly what he was up against when he set out before the beginning of the century to make himself into an English composer. 'Who Wants the English Composer?' is the title of an essay he wrote early in his career, and at the time when he wrote it it was a question that seemed to have no answer. Almost all the books written about contemporary music before, say, the middle 1930's, if they mention English musicians at all, tell one two things about the music of Vaughan Williams, and tell them so often and so emphatically that all sense of proportion about them was, for a long time, lost: that he collected folk-songs and incorporated them into his style, and that he made use of modal scales. There were two opinions as to the propriety of both these habits. More ink was probably expended in discussing the rights and wrongs of Vaughan Williams's use of folk-song material than on any other musical matter in this country since the turn of the century. Almost every musician recorded his views on the subject, from Sir Donald Tovey who wrote — 'Vaughan Williams composes with consistent nobility and in a style which it would be an impertinence to trace to its various historical origins,' to Constant Lambert who, in a book called *Music Ho!* compared the folk-song to the cult of the exotic and declared it dead and buried. Vaughan Williams was not, of course, alone in bearing this condemnation; Holst, Butterworth, Moeran and many others grouped under the banner of Cecil Sharp and the 'Folksong Movement' came in for their share of the blame. Contrary to popular belief it was not Sharp who introduced Vaughan Williams to English folk-song, for the collecting of folk-songs seems to have been a new passion that attacked musicians suddenly and simultaneously all over the country. 'I did not imbibe folk-song from Sharp,' writes Vaughan Williams, 'and when I first started collecting, in 1903, and began boring my friends with them I left Sharp out of the list because I thought he would not be interested.'

To the ordinary public, excited enough about music to read books about it, this general condemnation (for Tovey's attitude was exceptional) is puzzling. The very books that sneer at those English composers who refreshed themselves at this new-found spring of native melody, go on to eulogise any foreign composer who makes good use of his own country's songs. Has anybody ever read a word condemning Bartok's style on those grounds? or that of Kodaly? or Dohnányi? For what do we prize the music of Falla if it is not for the distinctive flavour given it by Spanish folk-song? Glinka and Borodin, Dvořák and Smetana have little of distinction in their idioms that is not the direct outcome of their various national backgrounds. We even like to believe that in the music of Sibelius we are hearing a distillation of Finnish folk-song — as if any of us would recognise a tune as Finnish if we heard it! It is only the English folk-song that is disreputable; to the English composer only is the enjoyment of his birthright forbidden.

The ground for objection to the use of English folk-song is, of course, that Bartok and Falla, unlike Holst and Vaughan Williams, come from countries where a surviving peasant population still hand down their songs from one generation to another. Our own folk-music is dead. Yet if that be so, may it not be like the grain of wheat that must fall into the earth before it can bring forth much fruit? We should judge the fertility of our folk-song tradition, not by any group of isolated rustics we may still find performing morris dances on a remote village green, but by the greatest symphonies and choral works of Holst, Vaughan Williams and the composers they influenced and taught. To them folk-song was a 'liberating influence' and helped them to throw off the shackles of nineteenth-century Teutonism.

C   R.V.W.

The folk-song controversy seems, at last, to have died. Indeed the folk-song has become respectable and musicians who, before, had sneered at those composers who came under its spell can now be heard learnedly discoursing on the subject even on the Light Programme of the B.B.C. The story seems improbable and fantastic to those generations who grew up since Cecil Sharp published his findings, whose early musical experiences included an intimacy with the *English Hymnal* or *Songs of Praise* or the *Oxford Book of Carols*. 'Dives and Lazarus', 'The Turtle Dove', 'Bushes and Briars', tunes long forgotten, are common property again. 'Everyone', says Vaughan Williams, 'must use the means that enable him to do his best.' It was the discovery of folk-song which, for him, suddenly set all other music in its right perspective, suddenly enabled him to realise himself, and he did not disdain to use it to the full. 'Integration' and 'love', he wrote, in *National Music*, are the only things that count in admitting folk-song to your music. In his own the integration is so complete that it is difficult to believe he can always be sure whether a melody is his own or whether it is traditional; the love so deep that when he is setting a folk-song he seems to be most happily expressing himself. Nowadays the situation of the English folk-song has so changed, it is so accepted and respectable, so much a part of our daily lives, that there are people who cannot abide the music of Vaughan Williams simply because they are tired of folk-song.

Vaughan Williams's use of modal scales comes as a direct consequence of folk-song, for folk-song, like plainsong, makes use of those ancient scales on which all music was based, by natural instinct and the human voice, before the exigencies of written music and civilised western harmony imprisoned all composition within the confines of the major and minor scales. To discover the modes one has only to go to the piano and, starting on each of the white notes of the octave in turn, play the eight white notes up from it. Each mode has, consequently, a different arrangement o intervals. The modes have strange and beautiful names — Dorian, Phrygian, Lydian, etc. — and the ones most common in English folk-song are the Mixolydian and the Dorian. Their use by

Vaughan Williams and other modern composers imparts to music a freshness and a mystery that has been too long absent from the music of the west.

Vaughan Williams suggests that the harmonic possibilities of these purely melodic scales occurred first to the nationalist Russian composers, and that he and his colleagues in the folk-song revival were, in fact, doing nothing new. This, their own particular revolt against the long tyranny of the major and minor scale, was only one symptom of a world-wide revolution. Schoenberg, abolishing all sense of key with his Twelve-Tone System, in which every semitone is of equal importance, was on a similar quest. Other composers, earlier, had experimented with the whole-tone scale. Vaughan Williams, catching Beethoven out in a modal cadence, goes so far as to wonder if that 'apostle of the tonic and dominant' had been about to enter into a new territory of greater harmonic freedom.

It is the use of these ancient scales that makes the work of Vaughan Williams sound both modern and as old as the art of music at one and the same moment. Teachers of harmony have always held that the use of the modes was permissible for melodic purposes only. On no account could they be harmonised. Dr Vaughan Williams ('recklessly oblivious of harmonic consequences,' as Grove describes him) disclaims, in the preface to his opera 'Sir John in Love', the ability to teach even elementary harmony, and goes his own uninhibited way, producing by such shocking and forbidden means the ravishing sounds of the 'Serenade to Music' and 'Flos Campi'. He strays still further from the straight and narrow path his masters vainly strove to keep him on, offering us without shame rows of consecutive fifths! Perhaps you do not tremble sufficiently at the thought; but in his autobiography the late Sir Arnold Bax describes the horror occasioned to his teacher and himself alike at the discovery of even one pair of them in a composition exercise. They are subversive of key and their use is considered licentious. They lead to a further dreadful error known as 'false relation'. It is the perpetration of this particular crime that makes Vaughan Williams's Mass in G minor so magically unlike any music ever heard before or since, and it is responsible for the peculiar alchemy of that great tune that intrudes so unexpectedly upon the jazzy first movement of the Symphony in E minor. The fluidity of key in his music carries us whither we least expect. It is extraordinarily restful to surrender to its guidance after centuries of knowing exactly where the next modulation is going to take us. We have been exhausted by two centuries of music written in two modes only; the sudden expansion of harmonic resources is like a draught of living waters.

I have written about these shocking and disputed matters from folk-song to its harmonic consequences only in order to put them behind me and forget them; for it seems that Vaughan Williams's name cannot even now be mentioned without provoking some discussion of them. He was determined to be an English composer, believing passionately that an international style of music would be as dead and colourless as Esperanto. But his Englishness is not derived from his love of folk-song only. It is bred in the bone and shows itself in the texts he loves to set to music — Skelton, Chaucer, Shakespeare; Bunyan, Herbert, Coverdale, Crashaw; Stevenson and Housman —in his knowledge of the Bible and his intimacy with the English country landscape. But his choice of teachers and his taste in other men's music show him to be in no way insular. He could never have become a follower of Percy Grainger — that composer who made a valiant but unsuccessful attempt to establish an anglicised vocabulary of musical terms to replace the Italian ones.

Our recognition of Vaughan Williams's musical Englishness does, however, seem to have raised some misconceptions. Again and again I seem to read that his music is restrained, reserved, unpassionate. Hubert Foss, who wrote the first book on the composer to be published, seemed able to hold this view even while noting an occasional extraordinary resemblance to Puccini — a resemblance that continually surprises and delights me, but which I would hardly have dared to mention if I had not found a reputable critic who agreed with me! 'About his music', wrote Foss, 'there hangs a certain mist of shyness, of tongue-tied inexpressive-

ness, only occasionally does he lapse into "take it or leave it"
assertiveness.' This view of Vaughan Williams's music seems to
me to be totally unreal. I have always wondered at the traditional
portrait of the Englishman, cold, unfriendly and phlegmatic, so
unlike the Elizabethan man, his forefather; so incapable, one would
have thought, of producing the wealth of poetry and literature
that speaks for him. Vaughan Williams seems to me to be no shyer
than John Donne, no more tongue-tied and inexpressive than
Shakespeare, Marlowe or Milton. The core and centre of his
power over me and over all who love his music is the romantic
and religious passion that soars into ecstatic melody alike in a love
chorus from one of the operas or in the great climaxes of the
'Tallis' Fantasia and the Romanza of the Symphony in D. His
ability to ascend with his lark always one climax higher than the
ear expects can be almost unbearable; and in the sweetness of some
of his lighter music is a quality that is, at one and the same time,
gay and heart-rending. Vaughan Williams's life-long habit of
early rising is, no doubt, partly responsible for the cool freshness
that bedews the pages of many of his early works, but because the
colour is delicate and the texture translucent it does not follow that
the music is cold. There is a passion in the early morning of the
'Pastoral' Symphony to match the blazing autumn colouring of
the later Pavane and Galliard from 'Job'.

But this is generalisation and to generalise about Vaughan
Williams is not safe. As in the case of Shakespeare or the Bible,
you can prove anything you like out of his long list of compositions by careful quotation. His perversity seems to be quite deliberate — as when he decorates a score with titles and quotations
and then begs us to ignore them. Whenever I find myself tempted
to make some definite statement about his music I do it with the
acute apprehension that nonsense will be made of it by the very
next work I hear. He has constantly been spoken of as writing
music that is 'tranquil' and 'serene' and the words seem appropriate to him and true until the next performance of the Symphony
in F minor or the Piano Concerto. If, having made ourselves
familiar with his love of the quietest regions of the English coun-

tryside, his devotion to the Church, his Elizabethan attitude to music-making, we feel it would at least be true to say — 'We will certainly find no jazz in the works of this composer ' — then, undoubtedly, in the very next we hear — in 'Job', for example, of all unlikely places! — there it will be, miraculously appropriated to his own ends. It is his ability to absorb whatever he chooses, without incongruity, into his own style that enabled him to turn his folk-song discoveries to musical account, with the result not so much of making his own music sound like folk-song, as of making folk-song sound extraordinarily like Vaughan Williams.

And now we must go back to the beginning of the century and the moment when English music began to wake out of its two hundred years' sleep; back to the untroubled time, before two great wars, that is more difficult to imagine now than any period of our more ancient history, and whose music, however tentative, however inexpert, has a freshness and delight that the present day, with its established and admired school of British composers, can never quite recapture.

CHAPTER III

1894 - 1922

*Songs of Travel : On Wenlock Edge : Fantasia on
a Theme by Thomas Tallis : The Wasps : Sea Symphony : Mystical Songs : Hugh the Drover : The
Lark Ascending : London Symphony : Four Hymns :
Pastoral Symphony*

It has been noticed monotonously by the critics that 'Toward
the Unknown Region' has a title that prophesied the way
Vaughan Williams was to go, almost as if, in selecting it from
amongst the Whitman words, he had baldly and deliberately announced his intentions. Dated 1905, this cantata was not his earliest
composition, but it must have been the first to make people
wonder if a new and very different composer had been found.
Written for chorus and orchestra, it was, in the words of a Stevenson poem he set about this time, 'a fine song for singing, a brave
song to hear.' 'Darest thou . . . walk out with me toward the
unknown region . . . no map there, nor guide, nor touch of human hand.' This broad inviting song was the first step on a journey
that led him further and further from the beaten tracks of his
teachers and contemporaries into the remote regions of harmony
and the uncharted regions of the mind. There have been times
when even those who followed his career with the most sympa-
thetic understanding wondered where he was going; other times
when it seemed as if he had retraced his steps and returned to an
earlier mood and style. It has always been impossible to predict
whether his next work will lead us to unknown desolate wastes,
or delight us, as he has so often, with a new and glowing variation
on the familiar landscape of home. There was a moment, round

29

about the composer's seventieth birthday, when it seemed as if the
wheel had come full circle and Vaughan Williams had settled to a
comfortable old age of composing music we could all understand,
but it proved only to be the starting-point of a fresh exploration
that invited us to follow to the bleakest regions music ever painted.
This latest departure cured everybody, once and for all, of the
habit of making prognostications about his future.

If we would understand his music we must attempt to make
this journey with him, and, to make our way plain, I am going to
divide it into the four stages into which it seems to me to fall. The
first comprises the early music in which Vaughan Williams, at
moments tentative and questioning, beckons us to his side that we
may consider with him the objects which give rise to his inspiration; the second in which he goes forward alone, caring not at all
whether we follow; the third when he returns with music that is
positive and sustaining, a solid edifice of achievement, warm and
sheltering. He has, in recent years, embarked upon a fourth stage
of his pilgrimage, in intention resembling the second, and of which
it is impossible to predict the length, the pattern and the outcome.

The fanfare challenge of 'Toward the Unknown Region' is a
tempting starting-point for this exploration, but history must be
respected and the beginnings sought a decade further back.
Vaughan Williams, an admitted pioneer among the world's composers, began life respectably enough. He began as was becoming
to a young English musician of the 'nineties, pupil of Stanford and
Parry at the Royal College of Music, as a writer of unexception-
able songs. To anyone who studies the writings of music critics
who remember that time it is obvious that these songs, for voice
and piano, were new and different and distinctive; but it is hard
for anybody who was born after the Great War to listen to them
with any sense of history, though it is possible to understand how
certain of his intervals may well have troubled the Edwardian ear.
So many of these songs have merged themselves into our national
consciousness that they seem to be now a part of the distinctive
background noise of English life, along with 'Sine Nomine' and

'Come Down, O Love Divine'. I could not possibly remember
when I first heard 'Linden Lea', 'The Vagabond' or 'The Road-
side Fire', or the more sophisticated art-song 'Silent Noon', but
when I discovered Vaughan Williams's music I found that they
had always been 'an unregarded part of my existence, like the
historic buildings that a Londoner never bothers to visit because
they are around him all the time. 'Whither must I wander?',
the first of his settings of Robert Louis Stevenson, has the date
1894 and is the only work of his I know that survives to us
from the nineteenth century; yet no simple ballad tune could
possibly carry more of a composer's personality than this most
stubbornly English of songs, written sixty years ago when musical
England was still in the grip of Teutonism. 'Linden Lea', over-
worked but none the less immortal, spun out of William Barnes's
dialect poem as if it were a folk-song with words and music growing up together, was written in 1900; both these melodies were
composed before 1903 when Vaughan Williams discovered folk-
song for himself. Both of them show very plainly that the overwhelming discovery was not for him so much a revelation as a
confirmation, for the spirit of English traditional melody was in
the marrow of his bones.

Nevertheless, there is something conscientiously polite about
these early songs, written before the free winds of Norfolk folk-
song had time to blow the formal harmony he had absorbed at
the Royal College of Music clean out of his system for ever. In
what we may call his 'Rossetti Period' he seems, to modern ears,
a very well-behaved composer. 'The House of Life', his first essay
in song-cycle form — he had written six, of varying degrees of
elaboration, by 1922 — captures all too successfully the lilies and
languors, the stained-glass airlessness of the Pre-Raphaelite
Brotherhood's paintings. Dante Gabriel Rossetti is hardly a poet
with whom Vaughan Williams would have been expected to find
much in common, but he captured the young composer's imagination for a time, during which the six sonnets that make up this
cycle were set to music, and a further four were woven into a
cantata — 'Willow Wood' — for baritone, women's chorus and

orchestra. Alas, we never hear it now. 'The House of Life' is a fascinating work to study for admirers of Vaughan Williams's later music, though I find it, myself, so painfully doleful that I can hardly bear to sit the six songs out. It is full of evidences of a style that was to come to maturity in later years; there is the tenderness for words that made Vaughan Williams one of the first composers to do in serious music what Sullivan had done in light — to prove that the English language was very good to sing; there is the same flowing beauty of line, familiar to those who know 'Down Ampney'; the incomparable shapeliness of phrasing. Here, for once, it is not the living shapeliness of the Cotswold hills where he was born that the songs recall, but rather the chilly contours of monumental masonry. Is it being wise after the event to feel in this collection of songs a striving, threatening to tear apart these careful sonnets at the seams and let the free wind of heaven in? The shapely lines of melody are dragged back to a respectable dying fall within the framework of contemporary harmony, but their impulse seems to be up and up, as if they were trying to break free and grow into the long questioning phrases that make up the counterpoints of the Symphonic Impression 'In the Fen Country' and the 'Pastoral' Symphony itself. In one song, 'Love's Minstrel', the composer explores a plainsong metre, seeming already to be at work on the breaking down of the tyranny of the barline. One of the six songs — 'Silent Noon' — perfect as an enamelled miniature, has achieved a separate life of its own. It is not easy for a singer to capture its breathless moment of suspense and it appears all too often in song recitals by inexperienced singers, to the complete neglect of its five neighbours in the song-cycle.

Written between 1905 and 1907, the 'Songs of Travel' are rough and uncut gems in comparison with the polished Rossetti sonnets. Stevenson was an outdoor poet and Vaughan Williams was able to fit his words with music that is fresh and breezy, though some of the breeziness is still self-conscious and of the indoor drawing-room ballad style. There are two song-cycles, of which the first is the better known and the second the more varied. They were written for baritone and piano, but some have appeared with an orchestral setting which seems too important for the songs and curiously softens the splendid jangling discords of the accompaniment. These discords, which fall meltingly from the woodwind and strings, sound delightfully biting on the piano, an instrument Vaughan Williams was to use less and less as time went on, until it reappeared as an effective and almost indispensable member of the percussion section of his orchestra. 'The Vagabond', a stirring ballad ('to an air by Schubert' the note surprisingly reads), has a full measure of this discordance, a marching bass, and a glorious modulation between the verses that afforded us the deepest satisfaction in school singing classes, where I believe I first encountered the tune — its masculine vigour hardly appropriate to a hundred and sixty girls in snowy white. The piano accompaniment of 'Let Beauty Awake' is intoxicatingly pretty in a conventional sort of way, and 'The Infinite Shining Heavens' is full of remote and starry wonder, but, alas, I cannot really enjoy the polite and popular 'The Roadside Fire', and was there ever a sadder song than 'In Dreams Unhappy'? It is sadder even than the Rossetti songs, and suggests that the young Vaughan Williams had his fits of melancholy like any other young man — a fact that very little of his later music will allow us to believe; for Vaughan Williams obeys his own injunction to the young composer — 'Look about you' — and his music, however it may reflect the problems of the world, is as little introspective as it is possible for music to be. 'Youth and Love' is sad as well, but the plain, direct 'Bright is the ring of words' is stronger and shows, as all these songs do, how admirably Vaughan Williams had already learned to set the English language for his singer.

About this time, when Vaughan Williams was collecting folksongs around King's Lynn, 'In the Fen Country', a Symphonic Impression of the Norfolk landscape was written. 'Composed 1904, revised 1905 and 1907, orchestration revised 1935' — we cannot guess how different is the version we hear now. It is a work of some importance, for it bears the outward shape of so many of his compositions — that of a gradual ascent from a grey, still quietness to a glowing climax and back again to silence. As

William McNaught said, speaking of the Symphony in D in 1943, Vaughan Williams's music deceives us into three stages of realisation — '(a) Isn't it time something happened? (b) It is happening. (c) It has been happening all the time.' 'In the Fen Country' is a truthful impression of that flat wind-swept East Coast, where the largest wild flowers in England grow and the most romantic wading birds inhabit, and which you either loathe, or love from the bottom of your soul.

In the next song-cycle he wrote — 'On Wenlock Edge' — Vaughan Williams added a string quartet to his voice and piano. The voice was that of the incomparable tenor Gervase Elwes and the songs were sung in 1909. The composer found, this time, a poet very congenial to his musical expression, though it is sad to record that his enthusiasm was not shared by the poet. The discovery of A. E. Housman created an unprecedented stir among the young composers of the day, particularly those who had found inspiration in the rediscovery of folk-song. The form of his verses is simple and his words are often tinged with a half-humorous bitterness that is also the very essence of folk-song stories. Upon the publication of *A Shropshire Lad* Housman was overwhelmed with requests for permission to set his poems to music. This permission, for the most part, he reluctantly and rudely gave, although he would never allow his poems to be reprinted in anthologies during his lifetime. When a friend asked him why, therefore, he permitted composers to set them to music, he replied — 'At least I do not have to listen to the songs.' Of his various interpreters George Butterworth has always seemed to me to be the most faithful and the most spontaneous. His 'Shropshire Lad' song-cycle has a homely simplicity and a certain bucolic clumsiness that is, surprisingly, missing from 'On Wenlock Edge'. Housman drew from Vaughan Williams a work that is, except in its gentle closing song, haunting and painful. The colouring is dark until the sun shines from behind the clouds in the last beatific verses of the final poem.

At the moment of its first performance the ears of the critics and the public alike were eagerly attuned to discover echoes of a

new French influence in this work, for it was the first to appear
after Vaughan Williams's sojourn with Maurice Ravel; and the
ear is wonderfully good at hearing just what it desires to hear.
Ever since the first impression, however, Vaughan Williams's
advocates have been busily denying that any such influence was
perceptible, though the composer himself admits, 'I came home
with a bad attack of French fever and wrote . . . a song-cycle with
several atmospheric effects.' He goes on to say, 'I could not have
written Ravel's music even if I had wanted to', and, indeed, no
composer has ever been more constitutionally unable to write
anything but his own music, no matter how many influences he
absorbed into his own style. The influence of Ravel was a crystal-
lising force. It imparted a new sharpness to the folk-song rhapsodies that followed naturally upon Vaughan Williams's Norfolk
discoveries. It was while he was writing these that he became dis-
satisfied with his ability to express himself. His style was lacking in
clarity and Ravel was the most economical and lucid of living
composers. It is recorded that Ravel was not unimpressed with his
unusual pupil but that, when Vaughan Williams packed his bags
and set sail for England, he sighed and said (with the understandable confusion about English titles common to all Frenchmen) —
'It is indeed possible that he may have profited from his visit, but
waiting there upon the quay will be Sir Parry and Sir Elgar, and
all will again be lost!' Ravel was wrong. 'On Wenlock Edge' is
clear and transparent in texture, and, though the influence of those
admirable Englishmen is faintly to be heard in some of the works
Vaughan Williams was to write in the years before the Great
War, Ravel must have lived long enough to know that all was
well.

The song-cycle opens with one of the 'atmospheric effects'
(after Ravel) an upward rushing of strings depicting wind — 'On
Wenlock Edge the wood's in trouble' — and the singer declaims
against a stormy background. The elusive little poem 'From far,
from eve and morning' —is next, its first verse hushed over a
simple piano accompaniment of spread chords. The strings creep
in for the second verse with magical effect. In its restrained

urgency the singer's melody is one of the loveliest and saddest Vaughan Williams ever wrote. 'Is my team ploughing?' is given a more dramatic setting here than Butterworth gave it in his song-cycle, and its climax is almost unbearable. The composer, rightly, one cannot help agreeing, took it upon himself to omit two of Housman's verses. The poet was outraged. Vaughan Williams replied that he considered himself at liberty, having first obtained permission to set the poem to music, to use as little or as much of it as he liked, provided that he did not alter its meaning. 'Moreover,' he wrote, 'I should have thought that anyone would have been grateful to me for refraining from perpetuating such a line as:

> The goal stands up, the keeper
> Stands up to keep the goal.'

The contrast between the two lads, the ghostly and the living, is dramatic, and there is a suggestion in the singer's part of this and others of the songs, that the composer of 'On Wenlock Edge' might one day be a considerable writer of opera. The hand that wrote it is plainly recognisable in 'Riders to the Sea', written more than twenty years later. 'Bredon Hill' is the longest and the most elaborate song. The piano represents the church bells in varying moods from calm and distant to menacing. 'I did not succumb to the temptation of writing a piece about a cemetery' the composer declares, speaking of the effects of his 'French fever', but in 'Bredon Hill', with tolling bells and its suggestion of the heavy tread of mourners, he puts at least one foot on this favourite territory of Ravel's and Debussy's. The 'coloured counties' are evoked in loving gentle music before the atmosphere darkens for the sombre ending to the poem. Between these two dramatic songs the composer has thrown the pleasant inconsequential setting of what is little more than an epigram in Housman's more charming vein — 'O when I was in love with you, then I was clean and brave — '. The instruments echo the singer's closing phrase — 'am quite myself again' — twice, in gentle irony. In the last song the optimistic Vaughan Williams that we know from the later music quite overpowers the sombre Housman. 'Clunton and Clunbury, Clungunford and Clun, are the quietest places under the sun' is written over the poem, and though Vaughan Williams does not set these words he conjures up a picture of those sleepy West Country villages in his peaceful melody. Weaving over a lazy triplet background, it rises for a moment into declamation and then sinks reluctantly and dreamily into a golden sleep. It is one of the composer's most beautiful tunes.

The 'Fantasia on a Theme by Thomas Tallis', destined to become the most frequently performed of all the repertoire of modern English music, was first heard in Gloucester Cathedral in 1910. Forty-six years after it still continues to appear in the London concert programmes about once a month, undated and fresh as if it had been written yesterday. The 'Fantasia' has a certainty and perfection that is astonishing in view of its early date, and it was to be a long time before Vaughan Williams wrote anything more of such measured deliberation and deep thoughtfulness, or, on the technical side, of equal confidence and finish. The 'Fantasia' presents us with the contradiction that seems to be inherent in so many of his works; that it is the purest and most absolute music ever written; that it is full of implications of an entirely programmatic nature. The theme is one of the nine psalm tunes, written each in a different mode, by Thomas Tallis, the Tudor composer who was master of William Byrd. This tune is in the third mode, the Phrygian, E to E on the white notes of the piano — the second and the sixth notes flattened. It was published in Archbishop Matthew Parker's *Metrical Psalter* in 1567. It can be found, unadorned, set as the tune to Hymn 675, 'Thou wast, O God', in *Songs of Praise*. Tallis died in the reign of Queen Elizabeth, having lived under four sovereigns and through years of religious persecution. Like Byrd, he was a Catholic, and remained steadfast in that faith, protected in his later years by the favour of the Queen, who cared more for good music than for religious persecution. I do not know if Vaughan Williams was brooding on the circumstances of the life of Tallis as well as upon his music when he wrote this Fantasia, but I am unable to listen to it without receiving a vivid impression of the darker side of Tudor times, the side we are inclined to forget amid the colour and poetry and gaiety. The Fantasia is modelled on the musical form of that name that flourished in Tallis's time, in the sixteenth and seventeenth centuries and then became extinct. It is set out for two separate string orchestras, one large, the second consisting of two first violins, two second violins, two violas, two 'cellos and one double bass, which should 'if possible be placed apart from the first orchestra'. A solo string quartet, composed of the leaders of each group of strings, gives sharpness to the debate. The serene beauty of the scoring, at times massive, reminiscent of the organ, at times ethereal, when a solo instrument soars in lonely purity against the darkness, has no parallel among string works. There is, indeed, no music in the world with which to compare this, the nearest to it in atmosphere being the collection of string Fantasias by Byrd which partake of the same remote and tranquil beauty but have no hint of its passion. The exposition of the theme is undertaken by both orchestras with the soloists playing with their accustomed groups. Five mysterious chords herald the theme, followed by that comma breath-mark whose presence in a score is almost sufficient to identify it as by Vaughan Williams. The violins sustain D, high in the leger lines, veiling the sombre entrance of the hymn-tune's opening phrase. This is repeated twice, interrupted by an undulating figure that has a large part to play in the ensuing music. The theme is now given out in full and repeated more emphatically with a decorative accompaniment by the second violins. Now the orchestras divide, the main body of strings returning to Tallis's first phrase to hammer it out with its four times reiterated note that is to play a dramatic part late in the Fantasia. The smaller orchestra, muted and mysterious, utters the undulating figure from the opening as an antiphon. The music dies away. Now the solo viola, with its grave and learned voice, begins to discourse on the second strain of Tallis's hymn. The violin takes over the discussion and all four soloists mingle their tones in restrained polyphonic disputation, while the orchestras each add their occasional comment. From the moment after their first interjection passion begins to suffuse the debate, the violin giving the first hint in its very next phrase, and, from now onwards, the music glows steadily warmer and warmer. Eventually both orchestras and string quartet unite for an impassioned climax of heartbreaking intensity. Here is Vaughan Williams in touch with heaven indeed, but with a heaven that implies the existence of hell also. The music sinks, as if exhausted, but out of this relaxation sounds a great chord, four times reiterated, as in the first phrase of the Tallis tune, heavy with doom. It drops away to be succeeded by another, and another, falling in pitch and intensity. Some of the lower strings quietly pluck out the opening phrase again and the violin soars up out of the darkness into a final calm meditation on the theme of the Fantasia, while the viola accompanies in elaborate cadenza. The orchestras, divided, bring the music down to peace again, the violin alone soaring away upwards while the other strings sink down to earth.

This Fantasia — a picture of the Tudor age that comes nearer to Marlowe and Webster than to Shakespeare — was twice revised by its composer, in 1913 and 1919. What its imperfections were we cannot guess. It is impossible now to imagine that he could want to change one bar, one note, of this deep thoughtful music, and it is hard to believe that it was written so early in his career, the growth, the architecture is so confident. It soars from firm foundations in a succession of majestic arches like the nave of an ancient cathedral.

The 'Fantasia on a Theme by Thomas Tallis' is probably the best introduction to Vaughan Williams for anybody who is not temperamentally opposed to 'holy' music. For anybody who is, there is always the Overture to 'The Wasps'. Some years ago I played this ubiquitous 'classic' to a highbrow musical friend, no ordinary listener like myself. After the first few bars — a very proper buzzing — he remarked disdainfully, 'Rather representational, isn't it?' By the second tune, the one that is a mixture of a martial rhythm and a joyful ecstasy, he could no longer keep his seat; by the end of the seductive middle section he snatched the record I was about to change, demanding 'that luscious tune again!'

D   R.V.W.

'The Wasps' ought by rights to be vulgar and blatant, its middle
section ought to be stickily sentimental, it seems to have all the
necessary ingredients; but Vaughan Williams, since 'The House
of Life', never succeeds in being sentimental and only rarely,
though he has made some notable attempts, in being vulgar. The
abiding freshness of this Overture lies principally in the quality of
its three tunes, to a varying degree modelled upon folk-song. The
first is a mere good-humoured bustling; the second begins as a
respectable march and then gets out of hand, leaving the curious
impression that it is not a far cry from 'For all the Saints'; and the
melting middle tune is an example of the sensuous love music that
Vaughan Williams keeps mostly for his operas and that is as un-
connected with heaven as it is possible for any beautiful music to
be. I am always irritated to see this cheerful work appearing in yet
another concert programme, but my annoyance gives place to
exceeding great enjoyment whenever 'The Wasps' begin to buzz.
The Overture is attached to a whole suite, made up of items out
of the incidental music for a Cambridge production of Aristo-
phanes' comedy which Vaughan Williams wrote in 1909. The two
succeeding movements, *Entr'acte* and 'The March Past of the
Kitchen Utensils', are of a delightful silliness, the composer in each
case appearing to be determined to construct the best possible tune
out of the fewest possible notes. There is a further *Entr'acte*, and a
Ballet and Final Tableau which makes use of the rhythms of folk-
dancing.

　　The 'Sea' Symphony, performed in 1910, was the first of that
remarkable series of symphonies ending (until he gives us a Ninth)
with the Eighth Symphony in May 1956. By now Ralph
Vaughan Williams had become Dr Vaughan Williams, to which
honourable title he has obstinately clung, never consenting to have
it displaced by anything more showy. The scale of the 'Sea' Symphony was appropriate to his new dignity, employing a very large
orchestra, two harps, organ *ad lib*, a large choir and soprano and
baritone soloists; lasting about an hour and a quarter, and being
the first fully choral symphony ever composed.

　　This monumental and admirable work depressed me not a little when I heard it the first time. There seemed to be so little in it that could possibly have offended one's grandparents even in 1910, although one of the composer's distinguished masters, Parry, while giving it a goodish notice, nevertheless declared the score to contain a number of 'impertinences'. Impertinent or not, there seem, in this symphony, to be more echoes of a kind that Ravel would have deplored than elsewhere in Vaughan Williams's work — a little of the breezy style of 'Sir Stanford', a noble tune that would not have disgraced 'Sir Parry' himself, and even at moments a suffusion of the rich colours of 'Sir Elgar's' musical palette. But the older I grow and the less earnest I become the more do I cherish this symphony, and, although there has been a fashion for decrying it as something too English to be artistic, I notice that its performances draw large and happy audiences. Singers adore it. Vaughan Williams never writes a dull part for the voice as anybody who has sung alto, tenor or bass in even one of his hymns is gratefully aware. Choral singing was the only vital part of English musical life during Vaughan Williams's early years. It is not surprising that his first symphony should be choral.

The scheme of the 'Sea' Symphony faithfully follows that of the classical symphony until its final movement. This is entitled 'The Explorers' and is of such length and magnitude that it seems to overbalance the work. Although the composer does not call any part of it an Epilogue, perhaps the second half of the movement might be considered to fulfil that purpose. If so it is the first example of what later became his invariable practice, of rounding off his symphonies with a movement that unifies all four into an indissoluble whole. All the same I cannot help wishing that he had amputated some of the last half of 'The Explorers' where his poet, Whitman, seems to get much the best of the bargain. In the early days of the century Walt Whitman came to rival Housman as a poet for setting to music, drawing from Vaughan Williams 'Toward the Unknown Region' as well as this symphony, and a setting of the 'Dirge for Two Veterans' that was, years later, incorporated into the cantata 'Dona Nobis Pacem'. 'Whitmania', as the critic Sydney Grew, who suffered it *in extremis* called it,

struck such diverse characters as Holst and Delius. His words gave
Delius the inspiration for 'Sea Drift', and Holst's 'Ode to Death'
is, perhaps, the loveliest music he ever composed.

The first three movements of the 'Sea' Symphony are in accepted classical form as strict as the words permit, but the movements have each their own descriptive title and each may be sung
separately, apart from the work as a whole. The first movement,
'A Song for all Seas, all Ships', is heralded by a great fanfare and
the chorus declaim the words — 'Behold the sea itself!' Then a
sweep of upward bubbling arpeggios in the orchestra reveals the
limitless horizons of the seven seas as if great curtains were thrown
up at the beginning of an epic play. The chorus set the scene of
heaving sea and the great steamers 'coming and going . . . in and
out of port'. Most of the themes in this prodigally tuneful symphony grow out of the first subject of this movement — out of
the phrase of the chorus's second sentence — 'and on its limitless
heaving breast the ships,' and particularly out of the three notes of
'limitless', a triplet in a bar of duple time. The baritone makes his
entry to introduce the second subject with a salty impertinent
tune — 'Today a rude brief recitative of ships sailing the sea,' the
kind of perky tune Vaughan Williams loves to invent for the
second subject in a solemn movement. The chorus take him up on
'of dashing spray and the winds piping and blowing' anticipating
the scherzo in the spray-drenched descriptiveness of their music.
Then follows, more solemnly, 'a chant for the sailors of all nations'.
It ends proudly, to be succeeded by another fanfare and the
soprano, announcing herself with the clarion call — 'Flaunt out,
O sea, your separate flags of nations!' leading the chorus into the
development section of the movement and a tender song for 'all
brave captains . . . and all that went down doing their duty'. It is
sometimes difficult to remember that this loving threnody was
composed well before the two wars whose sailors it now, inevitably, seems to celebrate. The principal themes are now recapitulated, after a big climax on the vision of 'a pennant universal', but
the chorus quietly return to their original song — 'behold the sea
itself, and on its limitless heaving breast the ships.'

The baritone is the soloist in the sombre slow movement —
'On the Beach at Night Alone' — a poem from 'Sea Drift', whose
music drifts mysteriously out of the darkness, glows to its peak of
radiance and disappears again into the night. The singer stands on
the darkened shore listening to the breakers 'as the old mother
sways her to and fro, singing a husky song', and ponders the
secrets of the universe. Hushed and mysterious the orchestra plays
alone until he makes his entrance, echoed by the altos of the
chorus only, who remain seated so as not to break the breathless
quiet of the moment. His song is little more than a monotone,
their repetitions a crooning lullaby. 'As I watch the bright stars
shining, I think a thought of the clef of the universe.' Pure description passes into visionary incantation, heralded by a change of key,
a more lively theme announced by the horns, and an even marching bass plucked on the lower strings — a descending figure of
notes, warm and hypnotic. The soloist and the whole chorus, now
on its feet, launch into an impassioned discourse:

All distances of place however wide,
All distances of time,
All souls, all living bodies though they be never so different,
All nations, all identities that have existed or may exist,
All lives and deaths, all of the past, present, future,
This vast similitude spans them.

Yet impassioned though their song may be, its feeling is subdued
by awe and wonder. They rise to a fortissimo but they remain
entranced, and it is the instruments of the orchestra who reiterate
the horns' theme in emphatic fanfare and soar above the chorus in
irrepressible descant who are the articulate voices. After the
climax, 'Tutta Forza,' the chorus subside, leaving the baritone
alone and unsupported this time by the altos, to murmur his
words of the beginning — 'On the beach at night alone . . . at
night alone.' Then he, too, abandons the dream to the orchestra,
who prolong it into an extended postlude, 'molto tranquillo,' that
begins with a sigh and relapses into the gentle rocking motion of
the 'husky song'; the muted horns and the woodwinds making
exquisite interjections.

The bright dazzle of the Scherzo is a sudden contrast, blinding as fierce sunlight after the dark. The title is 'The Waves' and it is announced by another, terser, fanfare, calling back the opening bars of the symphony. The music here is like the flash of sun on foam, the salt sting of spray against the cheek. Woodwinds rush up the scale with tingling trills, the triangle hisses and the strings shriek in the wind. One can almost hear the bosun's whistles and the orders cracked out by the master-at-arms. The movement is neat and formal musically; purely descriptive as to its words, and the soloists have no part in it. 'After the sea-ship, after the whistling winds — .' The principal theme presents the sea, invigorating and rough, changing every moment in the bright gusty laughing weather. Out of the seething cauldron of sound the Trio sweeps, like a great ship breasting the waves, a broad and noble English tune, the best and one of the final flowerings of that school of musical Englishness that provided the songs that every schoolchild knows. This tune is of the genus that includes 'Land of Hope and Glory' and 'Jerusalem' as well as the big tune from John Ireland's 'These Things Shall Be', and it is surprising that Vaughan Williams has not written more music in this manner. Into it, as a counterpoint between the phrases, the orchestra tosses a bar or two of a good old sea shanty — 'The Bold Princess Royal.' So neat is this bit of quotation that, if attention had not been drawn to it, those listeners who are for ever searching Vaughan Williams's music for folk-song tunes would almost certainly pass it by, and miss, earlier, an even less obvious insertion of the first phrase of another song — 'The Golden Vanity.' In the energetic recapitulation of the movement's thematic material the big tune is introduced again, this time in the orchestra, the chorus joining in after the wonderful sweeping theme gets under weigh. The movement concludes in a scurry of spray.

The vast final movement, to words from Whitman's 'A Passage to India', can stand by itself as an independent cantata. The poet contemplates the world, its restless, unsatisfied children, and then adventures forth on a new romantic quest into the unknown. 'The Explorers,' as the movement is entitled, furnishes the com-

poser with a theme after his own heart. He has been writing variations on it all through his life, whether the exploration was of this
world and the world to come in his many adventures with 'The
Pilgrim's Progress', or Scott's last journey, which began as the
background music for a film and grew, inevitably, into the 'Sinfonia Antartica'. The opening theme of 'The Explorers', for
chorus without soloists, 'O vast rondure swimming in space —'
has a tune which, it is surprising to discover, is identical with the
first phrase of 'The Wasps' Overture, miraculously translated to
solemnity. Tenors and basses alone introduce the first theme —
'Down from the garden of Asia descending, Adam and Eve appear —.' They are interrupted by a mysterious semi-chorus of
women's voices, sixteen in number, singing in four-part harmony,
distant and unaccompanied:

Wherefore unsatisfied, Soul?
Whither O mocking life?

faint and supernatural sounds, floating over the vast chorus and
orchestra and dying away until only the sopranos are left. Vaughan
Williams, mercifully, allows this breathtaking moment one repetition. Often he will throw an exquisite moment such as this into
one of his works, leaving one to pine for its repetition until the
next time the work is performed, possibly a matter of years. Such
is the way of contemporary music — but it is an artistic restraint
that can be very painful to the listener.

The symphony sounds as if it were about to end shortly after,
where, in an emphatic climax, the chorus sing — 'The true Son of
God shall come singing his songs —.' But far from being the end
of the symphony, this is the beginning of something quite new.
The chorus settle in their seats, the orchestra plays an animated
obbligato, and the soloists leap to their feet — the soprano, who
has not sung since the first movement, and the baritone, silent
since the second, with the words:

O we can wait no longer,
We too take ship, O Soul.

and the music, which from that point we expect to rise to a climax even greater, begins to slacken its vigour and fall apart into a looser texture. Whitman asserts himself. Not many of us in the 1950's are afflicted with 'Whitmania' and we find it difficult to share in the enthusiasm that sent the musicians of 1910 rushing to his poetry for their inspiration. It is possible that I might find myself enjoying the end of this symphony more wholeheartedly if only the soloists could be inaudible, but they seem to achieve an audibility unusual in English concert halls at this point in the score, and I simply cannot 'take' their habit of addressing each other as 'O Soul'. 'O Soul, thou pleasest me, I thee — ' declares the baritone; and surely the line 'thou pressing me to thee, I thee to me, O Soul' is every bit as bad as the goal-keeper lines of Housman Vaughan Williams so scrupulously refrained from 'perpetuating'. The singers start their long duet energetically enough, but after those unfortunate words they seem to drift to seas whose temperature is less invigorating. Though they declare emphatically enough 'O we can wait no longer!' they linger by the way a considerable time 'carolling free', chanting their 'chant of pleasant exploration' in an atmosphere that has warmed to one of palm-fringed isles and balmy breezes. It is a kind of heresy to liken any bar of Vaughan Williams's music to that of Delius, a heresy equally displeasing to the admirers of both composers, but this episode inevitably reminds me of the perfumed beauty of that musician's writing. Since his name has crept in I cannot resist retelling in Vaughan Williams's words what, in his *Musical Autobiography*, he refers to as a 'strange episode'. 'I burst in on the privacy of Delius,' he relates, 'who happened to be in London at the time, and insisted on playing through the whole of my 'Sea' Symphony. Poor fellow! How he must have hated it!' Delius, unlike Vaughan Williams, was never a patient listener to other people's music and his agony can be imagined! I like to think that this seductive passage, if, after nearly an hour, he was in a state to take it in, may have been a small compensation. 'He was very courteous,' Vaughan Williams goes on, 'and contented himself with saying, "Vraiment, il n'est pas mesquin." ' The languorous music of this duet for baritone and soprano is extraordinarily beautiful, but in a manner that, even on long acquaintance, still seems to me quite foreign to Vaughan Williams's mind and style. A solemn hymn-like episode — 'O Thou transcendent — ' is the signal for the chorus to return and the baritone follows with a solo passage. These are marked as optional cuts in the score, the mere existence of which surely suggests that the form of this vast movement has got out of hand. The solemn chorus is repeated to the words 'Greater than suns or stars, bounding, O Soul, thou journeyest forth,' and then, while the orchestra interjects a busy shanty of a tune, soloists and chorus cry:

Away, O Soul! Hoist instantly the anchor! Cut the hawsers!

in a triumphant finale to the symphony that has less of finality in it than of preparation for new adventures to come.

The words of this wonderfully satisfying episode might stand as a motto over all Vaughan Williams's future explorations in the realm of music and philosophy alike:

Steer for the deep waters only . . .
For we are bound where mariner has not dared to go,
And we will risk the ship, ourselves and all.

but in the years that followed upon the 'Sea' Symphony he lingered for a time upon the homely English shore and it was not until after his long enforced silence during the Great War that he launched out again toward his unknown region in the quest that was begun in music such as the 'Wenlock Edge' songs and the 'Tallis' Fantasia. Between the 'Sea' Symphony and the end of the war he contented himself with the composition of music that is robust and good-humoured, and that must, to audiences of the day, have sounded aggressively English. To this period belong many of the folk-song arrangements as well as the Ballad opera 'Hugh the Drover', the 'Mystical Songs', 'The Lark Ascending' and the 'London' Symphony.

'Five Mystical Songs', to well-known poems of George Herbert, is another essay in the song-cycle form. Although Vaughan Williams expanded his resources — baritone solo, chorus and orchestra — this seems a smaller work than 'On Wenlock Edge'. Where before he had magnified every implication behind Housman's words, so that the poet's brittle cynicism broadened into tragedy, Vaughan Williams now exactly matches his poet, writing affectionately, peacefully and making use of the rhythms that grow naturally out of the words. At this stage of his development, when he seems to have been writing with extraordinary happiness, he joins hands across three centuries with a poet who met his God familiarly in his own churchyard and rectory garden. A critic once said of Vaughan Williams that 'he sees Heaven open as the door of his own home', and the words could stand for the seventeenth-century parson-poet as well. It is true that the last song of the group, the stirring 'Antiphon' 'Let all the world in every corner sing, my God and King!' predicts the stern vigour of the 'Benedicite' to come and the bright fanfares of the 'Te Deum' for George VI's Coronation, but the substance of the music of these songs is gentle, plain and exceptionally pleasing. Herbert's prayer, out of the first song, 'Easter':

> Consort both heart and lute and twist a song
> Pleasant and long.
> O let Thy Blessed Spirit bear a part
> And make up our defects with his sweet art.

seems to have met with a ready answer. One is bound to believe that the composing of these songs must have given Vaughan Williams particular pleasure. The tune he called to birth for the last song but one, 'Come, my Way, my Truth, my Life', is an enclosed and private rapture, an incantation, as if, in turning the words over and over in his mind's ear, he made them glow of themselves into music.

I have had occasion to wonder, in the last few years, what would have been the course of this history if my introduction to the music of my favourite composer had been by way of 'Hugh the Drover' instead of the *enfant terrible* of the symphonies. Could it have been so exciting? Would it have struck the same chord of recognition with which Vaughan Williams himself maintains that we greet all our greatest experiences in art? I wonder; and on the whole I think I am relieved that things fell out exactly as they did. In 1942 I might have been too young and too superior for 'Hugh the Drover'. 'Hugh — ' is one of my more recent discoveries. I sat enraptured through it, when it had been revived, in 1953, at Sadler's Wells, where it shared the evening with the later one-act opera 'Riders to the Sea'.

At that performance I found myself wondering what would have happened to the history of what is sometimes called 'the English Renaissance' if Vaughan Williams had found himself a Gilbert in those early days. If the libretto had been witty instead of serviceable; if the story had been either more plausible or more wildly improbable; if the right people had been in the right theatre at the right moment; might we not have had a series of light operas to the credit of the nation instead of the great symphonies, the choral works, the songs and church music that are now our boast? It is a solemn thought. Alas, Vaughan Williams has never been sufficiently critical of his librettists, not even when the librettist was himself, thinking perhaps that the music would cover up all deficiencies. With the solitary exception of J. M. Synge, whose 'Riders to the Sea' was a perfect opera libretto with hardly a word that needed to be altered, none of the authors he has set to music have made good theatre. In the case of 'Sir John in Love' he battered *The Merry Wives of Windsor* into much better theatre than Shakespeare had given him to start with.

I am not proposing to take a walking tour through 'Hugh the Drover'. I hope it will reappear from time to time in the repertoire at Sadler's Wells. I cannot forbear, though, to list some of the passages that enchanted me, from the first chord of the Overture that, as likely as not, will make you jump out of your seat, to the final chorus when Mary bids farewell to her little Cotswold town for a life in the open with Hugh — a life I cannot quite convince myself will bring her the happiness she expects. The scene of the action is Northleach in Gloucestershire, a wool-market town about a dozen miles over the hills from Down Ampney, and the period is the Napoleonic wars. Out of the mass of interwoven folk-tunes, from sentimental to martial, that make up the crowded opening scene, I select as my own favourite the lovely air taken by the heroine as her cue for entrance — 'For I'm to be married on a Tuesday morning.' It is a clean fresh tune with the hint of wistfulness that is rarely absent in English folk-song, and it might well have made the basis of one of George Butterworth's rhapsodies — written about this time — or have served Vaughan Williams for the same purpose.

Vaughan Williams's modest attitude to the writing of those parts of his ballad operas which are undiluted by folk-song is well known. 'Where I could not find a folk-song to fit I have made shift to make up something of my own' he says in the note over the score of 'Sir John in Love'. In 'Hugh the Drover' he was forced to 'make shift' to make up a good deal of love music for Hugh and Mary, both solos and duets. Unashamedly romantic, the music bids fair to outsoar Puccini's climaxes and reminds me irresistibly of that most unexpected composer. Tunes of this order occur at intervals throughout Vaughan Williams's life; in all his love songs; in 'Sir John — ' and, most exquisitely, in 'The Poisoned Kiss'; in the luscious 'Pretty Bess' song from 'Five Tudor Portraits'; almost too sweetly in the 'Serenade to Music', and in parts even of 'The Pilgrim's Progress' where, one would have thought, such music had no business to find itself.

Hugh's 'Song of the Road', which sometimes appears in song recitals, is a fine virile ballad — 'aria' never seems the proper word for a song in a Vaughan Williams opera — closely related to the Stevenson songs. Sung over a realistic rhythm of hoof-beats it rises at the end of each verse to a broad romantic climax. This, the most 'English' period of Vaughan Williams's career, inspired many imitators, writing folk-song rhapsodies after his manner. None of them ever achieved the kind of tune he was writing here. Superficially it is easy enough to mistake snatches of these other English rhapsodies for early works by Vaughan Williams, but one could never mistake this kind of song for one by another composer. At this period, when the 'London' Symphony was being conceived, his head seems to have been full of more tunes than he could control. Mary's confession 'In the night time, I have seen you riding, riding — ' and Aunt Jane's slow, long-phrased lament 'Life must be full of care — ' are only two among the many in Act I.

In 1937 Vaughan Williams added a new scene to the opera, which became Scene I of Act II. It appears, however, to have been dropped again in most productions, and I refrain from investigating its pages in the published score, for fear of the delightful songs we may be missing. The opera is quite long enough as it stands, and is already decidedly thin as to the story.

What strange associations has the good old hymn tune 'York' for this composer? Majestic on the brass it opens and closes his opera 'The Pilgrim's Progress'. Here, in a context that could hardly be more different, it heralds the second act, played, rather fast, upon the tubular bells which represent the bells of Northleach church. Investigating this tune in *Songs of Praise,* where it is found as the setting of the Scottish metrical psalm 133, we read 'the chimes of many country churches have played it six or eight times in four and twenty hours from time immemorial'. That the belfry of Northleach church still plays hymn tunes I can testify. It was playing 'Immortal, invisible God' when I last bicycled past it. So I have little doubt that the bells still sometimes play the tune they played for Hugh in the stocks. Enchanting music floods around us in this final scene; Hugh's song in the stocks, interrupted again and again by the drunken singing from the tavern; love songs comic (when Hugh, stiff-kneed from the stocks, embraces his rescuers) and serious (when Mary voices her doubts — so justified I cannot help feeling — whether she is quite up to the outdoor life Hugh offers); the springtime freshness of the May Day carol, issuing so unexpectedly from the lungs of the deplorable butcher; the hilarious episode of the soldiers; these are pearls strung on a string and the knots between them are perhaps not always too securely tied. Surely the central jewel is the ensemble in which Mary, backed by the chorus, and interrupted by the voices of her father, her aunt and the rejected suitor, tells of her love for Hugh. Unless my ears deceive me this rapturous flight of song is identical in pattern of rise and fall and, at times, even identical in melody, with the sublime climax of the Romanza from the Symphony in D.

The distressing tendency among critics and public alike to treat a great composer's work as sacrosanct and never to allow him the joy of relaxation has led people to look askance at 'Hugh the Drover'. 'The philosophical element is unconvincing,' complains Percy Young. Well, yes, and thank Heaven for it! If 'Hugh — ' is to be regarded as a moral work on a level with 'The Pilgrim's Progress' and the symphonies it is a sad work indeed. If only the libretto had been a little more satirical, the story more wildly improbable, we would probably treat it as what I am sure it is intended to be — pure entertainment. Vaughan Williams is no pretender to earnestness. Writing of his (more earnest) friend and fellow-composer Gustav Holst, and of a different opera, he says: 'I never showed him my comic opera, because he would never have been able to understand how I could at the same time consider it trivial and yet want to write it.'

And yet — and yet — in spite of everything that I have written in its praise, in spite of my enjoyment, I am well aware that if I were introducing a friend to the music of Vaughan Williams I would reserve the delights of 'Hugh the Drover' until his conversion was complete. It does not illustrate the quality for which we most cherish this composer's work, his uncompromising honesty; the Englishness is, for once, a little forced; there are too many love duets; perhaps more than anything he has written it justifies his own accusation of 'amateurishness'. William McNaught, in his book *Music and Musicians*, has summed it up very fairly. 'The cause of its failure may lie partly in the unreality of the bluffness and heartiness and sentimentality dutifully assumed by a composer whose natural bent is their antithesis, and, for the rest, in the composer's excess of musical sensibility.' Before 1914 the composer's 'natural bent', revealed later in the 'Pastoral' Symphony, the Mass, and 'Flos Campi', was not apparent to the world; perhaps not even to himself.

If the drone of 'The Wasps' is condemned as representational,

then I doubt if the solo violin of 'The Lark Ascending' can escape
censure by the musical purists. The voice of this violin is heard
again and again on Vaughan Williams's pilgrimage, weaving calm
golden patterns in the midst of the drama of 'Job', soaring out of
the darkness of the slow movement of the Symphony in D,
spreading a magical warmth even in the bleak waste of the 'Sinfonia Antartica' The long threads of melody predict the 'Pastoral'
Symphony to come and, in their unfettered rhythm, Vaughan
Williams can be seen at work upon the establishment of another
freedom — freedom from the rigid and confining bar-line. The
title was taken from a poem by Meredith that stands at the head of
the music:

> He rises and begins to round,
> He drops the silver chain of sound,
> Of many links without a break,
> Of chirrup, whistle, slur and shake.
> For singing till his heaven fills,
> 'Tis love of earth that he instils,
> And ever winging up and up,
> Our valley is his golden cup,
> And he the wine which overflows
> To lift us with him as he goes.
>
> Till lost on his aërial rings
> In light, and then the fancy sings.

The small orchestra, supporting the soaring violin, paints a fresh
watercolour, filling in the background of quiet country landscape, the clear air, the sudden chill of wind; it provides also a
tune in the folk-song manner whose square-cut rhythm serves to
emphasise the wandering of the solo instrument, as if, for a moment, we had come from the free air of the hills to walk in a
Cotswold village. The music is cold and sweet, qualities found
together in music only too rarely. The orchestra fades away before
the end, leaving the violin to its lonely ascent, higher and higher
into silence.

The 'London' Symphony was performed in 1914, but altered
considerably at a later date. Vaughan Williams confesses that he

had been thinking about a symphonic poem! (the exclamation mark is his) about London, when his friend George Butterworth, to whom the work was dedicated, said 'in his gruff, abrupt manner, "you know, you ought to write a symphony."' This apparently 'stung' Vaughan Williams and he decided to 'throw it into symphonic form'. This rather drastic and wholesale-sounding proceeding may perhaps be responsible for the fact that the 'London' Symphony, though superficially conforming more nearly to academic symphonic form than any of his later symphonies, never quite manages to sound symphonic. Another reason may be found in the superfluity of tunes bubbling irresistibly in the composer's mind at that date. So many tunes forced their way into the 'London' Symphony that the finished work bears more resemblance to the nationalist symphonies of Dvořák than to the writings of any other composer in this form, though it is pleasant to notice that he never falls into the abominable habit, of which he accuses that composer, of writing 'five endings to each movement'. The 'London' Symphony is immensely popular with audiences, including many people who would shun any of the six that followed it. The composer is quite often to be found conducting it in out-of-the-way concert halls, so one may guess that he has a particular affection for it too.

The 'London' Symphony is a nice demonstration of the contrary ways of composers. Having thrown in Big Ben, sounds as of a street urchin playing a mouth organ (or must I, in view of later history, call it a harmonica?) and a vulgar and rowdy street band, Vaughan Williams seems to have been overcome with a belated remorse and begged that it should be regarded as music pure and unprogrammatic and its title be altered to 'Symphony by a Londoner'. But as the 'London' Symphony it has remained. London, of course, must have been a very different place in 1914, but even that knowledge does not help one towards a belief in Vaughan Williams as a Londoner. Nothing he wrote up till this work makes it possible to visualise him spending even one night in town; and I can feel no proximity to the boundaries of the L.C.C. when listening to this music, except, briefly, in the last movement.

The symphony has a prologue and an epilogue — the epilogue being one of Vaughan Williams's contributions to the evolution of symphonic form — and the Westminster chime on the harp divides the end of the prologue from the first movement, and the end of the last movement from the epilogue. So at least one of the 'landmarks' fulfils a legitimate musical function. The prologue leads one gently into a mood of anticipation. The first two notes are a rising fourth and this interval is prominent in many of the symphony's themes. After the half-hour chime on the harp the crash of the first subject assails our ears. It is chromatic and rumbling and depicts the roar of London traffic. The second subject has three parts, of which the first is an undoubted tango and the third a simple childish tune of great charm and felicity. After the noise of the exposition the development comes as an enchantment. The brazen and aggressive themes are dissolved out into threads of melody. Woodwinds weave in and out of the shining texture echoing each other and the harp makes a ravishing appearance. The crashing first subject is subdued to pianissimo for the recapitulation; the delightful second subject tune is recalled, turning back upon itself with an unexpected modulation into a brighter key. A flurry of jingles, triangle, harp and all the shining colours of the orchestra end this wonderful movement. It is a lovely example of first movement or sonata form, delightful to analyse. To trace, with the help of a score, every little phrase in the development back to its origin in the exposition, will reward the listener with the discovery that an apparently inconsequent collection of tunes is, in reality, an incomparably well-organised pattern.

The slow movement, like that of the 'Sea' Symphony, is built up of three sections, the first and last slow, and characterised by a desperately longing melody for the cor anglais, that begins with the rising fourth; the middle section quicker, a shimmering tissue of sound woven through with passionate harp arpeggios. I have always visualised this movement as a night picture, a Whistler painting, although it is actually to the scherzo that the composer has given the sub-title 'Nocturne'. The middle section of this movement is introduced by a graceful theme for solo viola, for whose consoling tones Vaughan Williams would seem to have a special attachment. The same phrase ends the movement — a movement which, for all its beauty, leaves me every time with an uncomfortable sense of unfulfilment.

The scherzo sweeps away all doubts in its scintillating triplet rhythm. I must beg forgiveness here, for I can bring no musical intelligence whatever to bear upon this delightful nocturne. At the age of three my infant son was introduced to it and instantly declared it to be full of trains. I am comforted to find that Hubert Foss heard trains in it too, as well as trams, which, I confess, we failed to find. Meticulously we went through that movement. Few pieces of music can have been subjected to such a toothcomb analysis. The record eventually wore out. Express trains thunder through the station without stopping; local trains trundle leisurely in their wake; points are crossed; in the darkness the lights of an approaching tube thread their way towards us 'like a bright needle in dark tapestries'; the station is suddenly empty, the last train gone. Outside the big terminus we meet the harmonica player. The street band plays its vulgar tune under the bright lights. In view of his injunction to regard this as music pure and unprogrammatic I tender my profound apologies to the composer. Undoubtedly he was not thinking of trains when he wrote this scherzo, but, alas, since hearing it I am unable to travel in any fast train without the third movement of the 'London' Symphony as my inevitable and, by now, somewhat monotonous companion.

The finale opens with a few bars of grinding discord almost prophetic of the Symphony in F minor. They give way to a serene and stately slow march, one such as might accompany the funeral of a great man through the streets and to the Abbey. The harp strikes the three-quarter chime and ushers in the epilogue which takes us back to the theme and mood of the opening of the symphony, through a glimmer of woodwind and strings. The instruments die away one by one into silence, indicated by the word 'niente', a word which appears, almost like a signature, at the end of nearly all Vaughan Williams's scores.

There is a blank space of eight years in the list of Vaughan Williams's compositions, a space that looks the more empty because the other years are so well and truly filled. But before the outbreak of the 1914 war he conceived a further cycle of mystical songs which were destined not to be sung until 1920. 'Four Hymns for Tenor, Viola and Strings' is a setting of poems by Jeremy Taylor, Isaac Watts, Richard Crashaw and Robert Bridges; the Bridges poem being a translation from the Greek liturgy. This cycle plainly points the way to a deepening of intensity in Vaughan Williams, to the sterner self-discipline that was to shape the music of the post-war years — the Mass, the 'Benedicite', the symphonies. Superficially less endearing than in the Herbert songs, the composer strikes direct to the heart of each separate poem, paying less attention to its formal structure in his fervent penetration of its meaning. In every work Vaughan Williams gives us there is something new, and in the 'Four Hymns' this white-hot passion burns clear for the first time. Up till this time only the 'Tallis' Fantasia could be described as the writing of a mystic. The lovely balance of tones — tenor, viola, strings — is the only concession to sensuous beauty; the vision, the rapture is all. Vaughan Williams is able to crystallise a sentence, a phrase, into music that so inevitably fits it that one hearing will fix its pattern in the memory for ever — thus 'But Thy word is a lantern unto my feet, and a light unto my path', years later in 'The Pilgrim's Progress', whose plain vocal lines often recall these songs; and here, so many lines of poetry, given their inevitable musical contour once and for all time. The hymns can hardly be expected to excite an audience that does not know Vaughan Williams's music; for those who do they seem a product typical of the composer's mind, at once passionate and restrained, urgent and tender.

During the war Vaughan Williams served as an orderly in the R.A.M.C.; later as a lieutenant in the Royal Artillery in France. As a medical orderly his daily chores included some floor-scrubbing — an exercise he found 'conducive of musical inspiration'. These inspirations he stored away in his head for the future, coming back from the war with a mind broadened and deepened not only by experience, but by the necessity of damming up his own ideas. When he came home, instead of producing the work reminiscent of strife and bloodshed that most of his contemporaries produced in the other arts, he sat back and, taking his time, slowly delivered himself of the quietest symphony ever written, the most delicate and individual expression of his genius.

Because the symphony is labelled 'Pastoral' there will always be a desire on the part of its hearers to set it alongside the 'London' as the other side of Vaughan Williams's picture of English life. But it will not fit there. The gulf between the second and third of his symphonies is immeasurable. Emotionally they scarcely seem the products of the same mind; technically they are poles apart. The composer who, before the war, flooded his music paper with a medley of diverse and enchanting tunes — tunes with a beginning, a middle and an end — now writes no tunes, as such, at all, but an unending, always changing pattern of slow melody that unfolds like a panorama of undulating landscape.

Where the movements of the 'Sea' and 'London' Symphonies gave us a separate picture, each one aspect of the subject seen from a different point of view and in a different light, the 'Pastoral' Symphony surveys one countryside, unchanging except slowly as the seasons change, or as the shadows lengthen over the hills with the passing hours. It is not a picturesque landscape, a smiling sunlit picture or a summer twilight such as Delius might have painted. Its colours are soft, green and brown and grey, its trees bare of leaves, its sky clouded; but it has something of the strength and promise of a ploughed field in its bare directness that is invigorating as a summer landscape cannot be. It is as if the composer, coming back from the years of war and noise and the constant companionship of army life, had suddenly found himself alone among the hills around his home in a silence so grateful and profound that, as well as the birdsong and the wind, he could hear the stirring of the sap in the trees and the movement of the roots under the earth.

The orchestra is a large one and includes among the more usual instruments a 'natural' E flat trumpet, a 'natural' horn, bass clarinet, celesta, and a soprano voice singing wordlessly from a distance. Each of these instruments, and indeed the entire orchestra, is used with such delicate economy that the whole symphony sounds almost like a work for chamber orchestra.

The 'Pastoral' Symphony makes few concessions to the popular idea of what a symphony ought to be. It is very much in one mood. It has, virtually, three slow movements and the scherzo itself is only marked 'Moderato Pesante', though it accelerates towards the end to a brief 'Presto'. The fact that the word 'tranquillo' is written no less than seven times over the music of the first two movements gives a clue to the symphony's total effect.

Something about this work inhibits discussion. Among those who know Vaughan Williams's music intimately the 'Pastoral' seems to inspire a special reverence. You would think, to hear enthusiasts discussing the symphonies, that this one was the universal favourite. Yet, for some mysterious reason, it is practically never played, and one is forced to the conclusion that it is being protected for its own good from the curse of over-popularity or the danger that its delicate bloom might fade with too much admiration, as if it were not far too deeply rooted in the soil for such a disaster to be possible. In ten years I tracked it down to only one public performance, when perforce, as they had embarked on the playing of all Vaughan Williams's symphonies, the concert planners had to include it in the Prom list. During those years there were a few broadcasts, I should guess about one every third year. It was thirty-one years before the symphony was recorded, beautifully, on a long-playing disc, but since the recording it seems to have been performed even less frequently.

What is there in the 'Pastoral' Symphony to make it unique in musical experience? It is not, I admit, an easy work to incorporate into a concert programme, and perhaps we ought rather to congratulate the concert planners on their good taste in omitting it, than blame them for ignoring its existence. The Albert Hall is no place for music like this; I do not believe the Festival Hall, where all its subtleties would shine out clear, has ever heard a performance of it at all. Applause sounds vulgar after the last distant note of it has died into silence. What music can follow it? Yet what audience would be content to end an evening's entertainment on such a note? Even in the matter of recording perhaps the powers-that-be were not so far wrong. Turning a record in the middle of one of those slow movements would utterly destroy their effect. An examination of some of the composer's methods in the construction of his score helps a little to explain its unique quality. Two illustrations are sufficient.

In the second movement there is a trumpet call. Let me quote William McNaught's essay from the programme of the 1952 Prom season. 'The composer directs that the call should be played on a "natural trumpet": that is, without modern valves. A "natural" trumpet, operated by lip-pressure, can play only those notes of the scale which were ordained by universal arithmetic long before mankind arrived on earth, and which were maintained in music until the scale was pushed and pulled about in order to make all keys alike. Equal temperament is what we call it; and equal temperament prevails throughout this evening's music but for these few bars. If present ears should find some of these trumpet notes "out of tune" it is because they have been listening too much to Beethoven and not enough to the music of the spheres.' I fear I cannot accuse myself of listening anything like enough to Beethoven, nor can I claim much acquaintance with the music of the spheres, though I have always fancied it to be not unlike some of the music of this symphony, but this clear call, which is in no way mysterious, but plain and direct, is to me the most exciting noise in all music (except that 'exciting' is not the right word for an experience so profoundly still). I do not remember that the 'natural' trumpet sounded out of tune to me on the first occasion I heard it, and familiarity with the symphony has now convinced me that it is all the other instruments that are, in fact, out of tune, but I will quote the words of A. E. F. Dickinson about this passage: 'The point of the "natural" trumpet,' he writes, 'is that all the notes played, being in the harmonic series of E flat, shall sound their true intonation, thus giving a peculiar purity of effect. I confess that my ear for one is incapable of appreciating this, the fifth note in the tune always sounding flat to me, not as the natural offspring of the fundamental E flat (of which it is exactly, indeed, the seventh overtone), but as a flat D flat. I do not suggest that the composer is mistaken in employing a natural trumpet, but that he is mistaken in supposing that ordinary D flat sounds any less "natural" than "natural" D flat, to ears habitually used to equating the two.' The science of overtones or harmonics is altogether above the heads of the ordinary listener, but I quote this passage as an illustration of the mysterious and primitive means to which his search for the exact truth has led Vaughan Williams in this symphony.

Secondly, there are the famous passages for solo soprano, sing-ing wordlessly, that open and close the last movement. Sugges-tions have been made of meanings hidden here; the voice of Nature herself; a Wordsworthian shepherd boy? I am uncon-vinced. There are many solo tunes and phrases throughout this work, from the plaintive cor anglais of the first movement to the natural trumpet itself and the violin and viola. Each plays music that is vocal in line, as eminently singable as the notes given to the human voice. This is the normal behaviour of solo instruments in a Vaughan Williams score, and I judge that his soprano is no more human, no more charged with meaning than any one of these momentary soloists. It happened that the context of the last move-ment required a quality of sound that nothing but the human voice could supply. Vaughan Williams did not hesitate to use it any more than he hesitated to use his 'natural' trumpet.

Therefore we have in the 'Pastoral' Symphony the most sensu-ous possible arrangement of musical sounds; not sensuous in the manner of Delius or Bax who loaded their musical palettes more richly from the spectrum of orchestral colour, but sensuous be-cause each instrument is allowed to speak clearly in the full per-fection of its own particular quality. This is an epicure's symphony. Yet the impression it gives of sharing chamber music's intimacy is misleading, for there is immense power behind the music, the power of a broad river flowing deep and inevitable to the sea under an untroubled surface. The slow themes push their way upwards with such potentiality for growth that one is left at the close of each of the three slow movements convinced that, had he wished, Vaughan Williams could have gone on developing them for ever.

Under a soft wavering figure the 'cellos and basses, reinforced by chords on the harp, announce a quiet but strong and promising theme. The solo violin, 'tranquillo', plays a graceful melody that is taken up and echoed by the oboe. The soft light of the opening of the first movement shows how much, consciously or unconsciously, Vaughan Williams had learnt from French music — the 'points of colour' in which, he tells us, Ravel had taught him to orchestrate. The cor anglais plays a plaintive, questioning phrase, taken up by the violin; but the clarinet counters with a flowing melody that restores the momentarily lost tranquillity. These various themes are combined to build a climax after which the haunting lament of the cor anglais is repeated and may be said to have the last word. The sadness of this music — for that these peaceful themes are sad is undeniable — has a quality all its own. Vaughan Williams has far too positive a nature to indulge in romantic melancholy for its own sake. The 'Pastoral' Symphony is saturated with the sadness that resides inescapably in all natural beauty, in much the same way as Constable's paintings are dominated by their rain-bearing clouds; but the sadness of the themes is quite logically traceable to the inherent wistfulness of the modes in which they are written and to the pentatonic scale. It is a mood of melancholy that dominated the music of the Tudors, although the 'Pastoral' Symphony shares little with them but mood and the modes.

The slow movement proper comes second, its quality best defined by the composer's choice of instruments — woodwind, strings, four horns, the 'natural' trumpet and horn; no other brass, no percussion, no harp. Except in some solo passages the strings are muted throughout; the horns for most of the time. Over a dark background of strings the horn gives out a theme, sounding hollow and bare after the lush tone of the first movement. A mysterious string passage, rising, leads to the theme's repetition by an oboe and a clarinet. There is a silence. The strings resume their dark muttering and the viola announces a second theme of great tenderness, which is taken up and handed from instrument to instrument. This quiet meditation leads to the trumpet call which is the core of the movement. Though as strange as any sound in civilised music it is neither remote nor mysterious, but clear and direct. The trumpeter, operating his instrument by lip pressure alone, stands out, making the surrounding orchestra seem, suddenly, mechanical and urban; momentarily dissolving the walls and roof of the concert hall and letting in the skies. The movement speaks an emotion as profound as any the composer has expressed in music, but its atmosphere is temperate. We have come down to the bare bones of musical thinking.

There seem always to be dancing feet, heavy or light, in a Vaughan Williams scherzo. Across his empty landscape figures begin to stray. All the percussion come in to assist this rustic dance, including the celesta. The relative speed comes as a relief in this slow symphony. The opening is a galumphing measure, joined presently by a staccato march-like tune. A flute, as if played by some elfin creature, skims high above the general bustle with a lilting phrase. The trio rises 'naked and unashamed' (as Vaughan Williams once described Holst's orchestration) on the brass — a bright and splendid tune and one that must have delighted that composer, whose own brass writing has never been excelled. The scherzo is recapitulated and the trio recalled. Suddenly the rustic carnival dissolves, giving place to a coda of shimmering speed and delicacy — 'sempre pianissimo e leggierissimo.' Vaughan Williams has confessed to fairies in this Scherzo though he denies the human element most people are convinced they hear. For me this wonderful movement contains all of *A Midsummer Night's Dream*, Bottom and his 'rude mechanicals' in the trio tune, Puck in the flute theme; and, in the headlong fugal coda, which combines the staccato dance with the flute solo and its own opening theme, Oberon, Titania and all the fairy crew.

Over a bare drum roll the soprano sings her leisurely bar-less solo, leading the orchestra into one of those slow build-ups that

Vaughan Williams loves to contrive. He leads us from silence to the summit of his rounded hill, shows us the 'coloured counties' or bids us survey the 'infinite shining heavens', then leads us gently down upon the other side. In this movement the intrusive word 'tranquillo' is absent. Beginning 'lento' and continuing 'moderato maestoso' the music is disquieting, though, if comparisons are possible, the most beautiful of all. After the soprano's, another theme, 'cantabile' is introduced, apparently serene but, when it is taken up by the lower strings, revealing a longing, a divine discontent only matched by the slow movement of the D major Symphony years later. An agitated tremolando string passage leads to a quick, strident quotation of the soprano's theme, first on the cor anglais, then the violin. This almost desperate passage leads unexpectedly into a recapitulation of the 'longing' theme over a translucent background of harp, purling like a clear brown stream over pebbles. The flute claims the theme and floats it graciously over the loving accompaniment of harp notes, giving it its own particular and captivating twist, and so leads into a passionate unison restatement of the soprano's tune, fortissimo on strings and woodwind. The movement finishes in a typical Vaughan Williams slow ascent to a radiant climax over a glorious passage in which the whole orchestra runs up and down the scale in counterpoint, and an equally typical descent to near silence. The soprano, this time veiled by a high note on the violins, quietly repeats part of her opening theme.

I have ended this chapter with the 'Pastoral' Symphony because, although it appeared after a gap of years and is enormously more mature and original than anything Vaughan Williams wrote before the war, it seems the logical rounding off of a period that also included a 'Sea' and a 'London' Symphony. In these symphonies, with 'Hugh the Drover' and the folk-song rhapsodies and the historic splendour of the 'Tallis' Fantasia, he painted a complete picture of England — an England before the Great War that my generation finds hard to visualise. Is there a trace in the regretful beauty of the 'Pastoral' of a nostalgic valediction for that vanished world, as if he had caught a mood from Delius? If there is, then it is a mood only, for the 'Pastoral' has a far from Delian economy. Every note carries its full weight of meaning, both as part of a highly organised musical pattern, and as an essential of the composer's vision; every thought is barely but sufficiently clothed with music. With the composition of this symphony, unique in form, Vaughan Williams shed every lingering trace of the 'bluffness and heartiness and sentimentality' that disfigure parts of 'Hugh — ' and are not entirely absent in the two previous symphonies, and became, once and for all, the composer that we know today.

CHAPTER IV

1922 - 1935

Mass in G minor : Violin Concerto : Flos Campi :
Sancta Civitas : Riders to the Sea : Sir John in
Love : Benedicite : Job : Magnificat : Symphony in
F minor

The second stage of our journey alongside Vaughan Williams begins in 1922, the year of the 'Pastoral' Symphony, and ends in 1935, with the terrific Symphony in F minor, his fourth. It is a period of adventure and discovery, spiritual and technical alike; and the works written during these thirteen years have an astonishing variety. Up till this moment it has not been difficult to follow Vaughan Williams's growth as a composer. The influences of folk-song and the music of the Tudor polyphonists, acting upon his individual inspiration, were shaping a style that found its first complete expression in the 'Pastoral' Symphony. From this point onwards Vaughan Williams becomes the unpredictable composer we now recognise him to be. From this point onwards his path begins to be littered with a vast accumulation of discredited prophecies that (one might almost suspect intentionally) he proved one after another to be wrong, and which now make delightful reading. To this period belong at least three of the masterpieces of modern music — the ballet 'Job'; the suite 'Flos Campi' and the Symphony in F minor — three works as different in subject, form and style as could possibly issue from the mind of one man.

In the days before the 'Pastoral' Symphony had been performed Vaughan Williams had been accused of writing music 'with his boots on', and perhaps, looking back on the first two symphonies, 'Hugh the Drover' and their attendant rhapsodies and songs, one can detect a spice of truth in the suggestion. After all a man needs boots to climb the Cotswold hills, though he may forget their existence, if they are well-fitting, when he stands to listen to the bird-song pouring from the sky above his head. There has certainly never been a smell of midnight oil about his music.

But the Mass in G minor, composed simultaneously with the 'Pastoral' Symphony, does not sound like the work of a countryman, though it shares the quiet economy of that symphony, its shapely lines, above all its quality of worship in stillness. It was written for the choir of Westminster Cathedral, and it is an odd fact that this, perhaps the most successful of all modern English settings of the Mass, should be the work of so Protestant a composer — a composer obsessed for so many years by the writings of John Bunyan. It is even stranger that Elgar, who was born a Roman Catholic, never attempted a setting.

The Mass is for double choir and soloists — soprano, alto, tenor, bass — reproducing thus in human voices something very like the arrangement of strings in the 'Fantasia on a Theme by Thomas Tallis' (double string orchestra and string quartet), reminding us once again how vocally Vaughan Williams writes for instruments, how instrumentally he can use his voices. The Mass is in the pattern of Byrd and his contemporaries, unaccompanied and polyphonic in texture, unextended, undramatic and plainly intended for its proper use, whether in Latin, or translated for the Anglican Communion. It is heard at its best in church and is not a really happy work for the concert hall, having nothing in common with the big Masses of Bach, Beethoven and the romantic composers. Parry would have discovered far more 'impertinences' in this plain, sweetly austere score than he found in the ample 'Sea' Symphony. The modes dominate it, for all its respectable title 'G minor', the flattened sevenths which so vexed Stanford are triumphantly in evidence, and the whole work is built up on a structure of 'false relation'. The ordinary listener, unconscious of these crimes, is one up on the musician, and able to abandon himself to the music without prejudice.

It is these very 'impertinences', together with the glowing and glorious counterpoint, that give the music its undatable quality. On a first hearing, particularly during the Kyrie, with its undulating contours, the ear places it instinctively in the 'golden age' of Byrd and Palestrina. Listening further it detects the urgent contemporary voice through the deliberately archaic polyphony. It is not easy music, no easier than Byrd or Palestrina, and demands, like them, an intensity of concentration that the classics and most modern music do not demand. Moreover, like the music of those early masters, it is not subject to the gradual softening that time brings. It is no more easy to understand it in 1956 than it was in 1922 or will be in fifty years, and no more difficult. It needs to be heard with ears washed of all historical association. Sir Richard Terry, who had commissioned the work, sums up its effect in a letter to the composer: 'In your individual and modern idiom you have really captured the old liturgical spirit and atmosphere.'

The Gloria dances with an unearthly radiance, restrained though be it, recalling the far-off mystery of the dancers in Holst's 'Hymn of Jesus'. The swaying chords, high in the register of the soprano's line, drift sweetly down like snowflakes on each repetition of the word 'Sanctus'. The Credo is singularly plain, dwelling for no length on any one article of belief. The central core, 'qui propter nos homines —,' is more personal than the rest of the music, the reverent Incarnatus rising on a plain progression of notes charged with wonder on the words 'and was made man'. The 'Amen' is of great splendour. Perhaps the Agnus Dei is the part of the work most typical of its composer, the urgent voices, solo or in chorus, sending up their appeals for peace with a strained intensity over the Misereres, which repeat the lulling pattern of the Kyrie. The Credo and Sanctus from the Mass in G minor were sung during the Coronation of Her Majesty Queen Elizabeth. In that service, which is practically an anthology of all possible styles and periods of English church music, it stood out from the rest in a simplicity that was almost forbidding. I asked Boyd Neel, who had been one of the conductors at that service, what in all the music had impressed him most. Without hesitation he answered, 'The Amen from Vaughan Williams's Creed.'

For me the Mass in G minor is as difficult a work as any Vaughan Williams has written. I cannot say, even now, when it is available on records, that I always enjoy it. One day it will pass icily over my head; the next, perhaps, I become enfolded in the hypnotic beauty of its counterpoint. In neither instance can I listen with anything approaching intelligence. In this work, which is more than usually woven throughout by his own harmonic vocabulary, I find it very difficult to recognise Vaughan Williams at all. The explanation may well be that here, for the only time in his life, he was writing as a Catholic. His approach to heaven is through veils of incense as well as over centuries of history. He is not on his familiar home ground where, in the Herbert songs, he met with God; nor is he assaulting heaven's gate with stirring psalms. It is in the most personal moments of the Credo, the Incarnatus and the Crucifixus, and in the urgent appeals of the Agnus Dei, that his voice is clearest, rather than in the submissive beauty of the Kyrie and the gentle Benedictus.

In 1925 Vaughan Williams published two works — 'Flos Campi' and the Concerto for Violin and Strings, originally called the 'Concerto Accademico'. The title was evidently forbidding. I can find no other explanation for the fact that it is hardly ever played. It seems miraculous that it contrived to get itself recorded. Vaughan Williams has a habit of trying to withdraw the descriptive titles and quotations with which he instinctively decorates his scores. Invariably he does this much too late. Who, for instance, if they ever read it, will forget the quotation from *The Pilgrim's Progress* that used to stand above the Romanza of the Symphony in D? Our memories are better than he would seem to think, and we are left bewildered sometimes as to his real intentions. Personally I intend to go on calling this concerto 'Accademico'. I like the name. I grew fond of it under that name. But I admit I am puzzled as to how it got there, and can only ask, with Donald Tovey's analysis — 'Why Accademico?' That most worthy of all musical publications, *Grove's Dictionary*, refers to it as 'the most un-academic of concertos'. If there is anything at all academic in this fresh little work, it is only the efficient fulfilment of its own strict and self-imposed demands. It is a small work, following the pattern of an eighteenth-century concerto, and recalling Bach by its self-sufficiency and the contour of one or two of its tunes; never, though, by its atmosphere, which is out-door and breezy. This is the first work we have encountered yet that is entirely innocent of programmatic suggestions, and it is worth studying, for this fact alone, even if, at a first hearing, it does appear forbidding. Here, if anywhere, Vaughan Williams was writing to please himself alone, and writing with his mind empty of all but musical considerations; his contemplation was for the possibilities of interwoven phrases, not of some outside subject that suggested music to his mind. The score is the neatest and most intricate picture of musical patterns imaginable, beautiful to look at, tidy as a Brandenburg concerto; and this is not always the case with a Vaughan Williams score.

The texture of the music is limpid as a water-colour. The instruments, it is true, are those that play the Tallis Fantasia, though differently arranged. It is strange to think that strings alone can produce this clear picture and that dark tapestry. And how differently does Vaughan Williams use his solo violin from most other composers! There is no bravura in this concerto and no show. The concerto as a form has not attracted him very often. In his music the violin preserves a fresh, cool, virginal voice, and the romantic emotion with which most composers endow it he reserves for his viola. He has written nothing to endear himself to the virtuoso violinist.

The first movement starts off a firm 'allegro pesante', a favourite measure of the composer's and one that always calls forth 'something characteristic' (as his teacher Parry would have called it). There is no time for his long questioning phrases here, but no excited hurry either: simply a brisk little trot. The solo violin starts off in unison with the other violins, as if to warn us that there is going to be no room for the usual concerto rhapsodisings and no showing-off. It is soon playing a cadenza, but firmly marked 'strict time'. It introduces a secondary tune in country dance rhythm which fits nicely into the trot, and the two tunes are worked together with a variety of contrapuntal device. But no sooner have we settled down to the continuance of this busy movement than the violin draws three separate strands of lilting cross-rhythm over the square-cut measure. Their effect is mysterious in the extreme and quite breathtaking. The orchestra does its best to pull things together, but something has been let loose and the solo violin, after a brief attempt to resume the former measure, breaks into smooth running rhythm over a Bach-like counterpoint from the strings. The development has a contrapuntal flow, interrupted occasionally by impatient reassertions from the trot. The entire movement seems to be a struggle between two types of rhythm — the square-cut and the streamlined. Eventually the violin achieves a streamlined cadenza which leads into the recapitulation. The briskness returns, the matter-of-fact bustle; we are back where we were before. The enchanting cross-rhythms cut across the texture, all three this time strung into one long phrase; but, as if we had dallied too long over the development, or the violin had wasted time on its cadenza, we are abruptly hurried into a terrific 'presto' which winds up and breaks off the movement before we know where we are.

There is nothing more purely musical than the 'adagio' that follows. It seems to belong to no age, no country, no musical 'school'. It is quiet, restrained, aloof, unsentimental, untinged with romance; but at the same time direct, flowing and gentle. This is Vaughan Williams at his most personal and this music finds its comparison in the works of Byrd and Bach. The solo violin, echoed by the first violins, traces long lines of undulating melody over a two-note 'ostinato' given to the second violins and, later, the violas. All but the 'cellos and the solo violin are muted throughout. The score, like the 'Pastoral' Symphony before it, is inscribed in several places 'tranquillo', beyond which description there is no need to go.

The finale is a lively and unforbidding 'presto' in which a number of themes of conflicting rhythm are mixed up with a snatch of a jig from the drinking scene of 'Hugh the Drover'. The exuberance of this movement dies to a respectable finish, with a quieter

F   R.V.W.

contrapuntal passage. When we think it is all over, suddenly the
solo violin returns, and takes a bow all alone, playing a cadenza
in strict time 'sul tasto' — on the fingerboard — in the most ami-
able and fantastic manner. It is neat and unexpected, and how little
music ends in any but the most obvious way?

How to convey the charm of this little concerto? To speak of it
truthfully is to confess that it lacks colour, lacks passion and is thin
in texture — three large defects to the ears of many a listener. But
if I were invited to one of the B.B.C.'s desert islands, accompanied
only by a gramophone and eight records, this concerto would be
the first music I would choose to pack. I fell in love with it at first
hearing and have not found it lose one note of its appeal after an
infinite number of repetitions. It is of all the works I know one
of the most lasting and companionable.

The music of India, which very few of us know very much
about, is based, not only on a different set of scales and modes
from western music, but is governed by a number of rules that
seem to us to be arbitrary and curious in the extreme. One of these
rules dictates the time of day at which it is permissible to play
tunes in a given mode. The Indians have morning modes and
evening modes, and to play a tune in a morning mode in the evening, or a tune in an evening mode in the morning would be as
gross a breach of taste as, for us, to play a jazz number in Westminster Abbey. No such rule applies to our music. Yet there is no
doubt about the morning freshness of 'The Lark Ascending' or
the Concerto 'Accademico'. Nevertheless we are content to listen
to them, for the most part, in evening concerts. 'Flos Campi',
published in the same year as the concerto, is undoubted evening
music. I cannot imagine the possibility of hearing it before the
light begins to fade. Vaughan Williams, who writes such bracing
outdoor tunes, such cool melodic patterns, the air of whose land-
scapes has so often a decided nip, has, in this short score, written
not one phrase, one note, that is not vibrant with warmth. It is a
suite for viola, with small orchestra and chorus, and to that solo
instrument Vaughan Williams allows all the passion he denies his
violin. There is an odd huskiness at moments in the voice of this

viola. It is singularly masculine. Women are often good viola players, but it would not seem quite proper to have one play 'Flos Campi'.

There is quotation trouble in this suite, which would never have arisen if, at some time in the past, the composer had not adjured us to take little notice of them. This is asking a good deal, for 'Flos Campi' is short, the quotations are six in number, one for each movement, and to make them even more prominent, they are written out both in Latin and in English. They come from the 'Song of Solomon' in the Vulgate version and are chosen in such a way that it is tempting to construct one's own scenario out of them. There are two opinions, of course, as to the meaning of this Old Testament book. Do you prefer to regard it, as was once the habit, as an allegory of God's love for His Church; or do you accept it as a collection of songs, more or less erotic, from a Jewish wedding feast? Vaughan Williams has given us no clue to his opinions. He has simply given us the music. It is for each of us to make up our own minds upon the interpretation that seems nearer to the truth, or to accept the music without interpretation.

Frank Howes, in his analysis of 'Flos Campi' in the *Musical Pilgrim* Series comes down upon the side of the love songs. He describes the 'stuff of the music' as a 'progress from a keyless, rhythmless, arabesquelike melody signifying desire and longing for the beloved, to a diatonic, rhythmic, almost march-like theme, worked contrapuntally and in canon and imitation expressive of fulfilment'.

'Flos Campi' is a suite, but it is played without a break, and it is not easy without a score to detect where the movements join. A continuity of emotional impulse carries the music through from beginning to end. The orchestra is strictly limited; not more than twenty strings; only one each of the wind; a chorus, that sings wordlessly, but on specified vowel-sounds, of not more than twenty-six voices. In addition are the instruments that add colour of an exotic kind — celesta, harp, triangle, cymbals, drum, tabor. There is economy in this score, but Protestant plainness has fled to the four winds.

'As a lily among thorns, so is my love among the daughters. Stay me with flagons, comfort me with apples, for I am sick of love.' The oboe, in counterpoint with the viola, play plaintive strains, each in a different key. The rhythm is indeterminate. Even so early, before the chorus or the colourful instruments have made any contribution, the atmosphere is curiously oriental, though the composer does not seem to be employing any definite tricks to assist its creation. The second movement bears as its title the most famous quotation from the book, 'For lo, the winter is past, the rain is over and gone, the flowers appear on the earth, the time of the singing of birds is come, and the voice of the turtle is heard in our land' — a quotation whose appeal to Vaughan Williams's mind is so obvious that it was bound, one feels, to find some illustration in his work before he grew much older. The music broadens, settling into something nearer to accepted tonality; the women's voices undulate on a dreamy figure of notes; the viola plays a long and meditative song, and the picture of spring in some un-English countryside becomes vivid, over a weaving background of harp arpeggios, threaded, towards the end, with notes from the celesta. But the viola's quest is too urgent to be interrupted long by visions of pastoral delight. Passionate and impatient, it sets out upon the third episode, 'I sought him whom my soul loveth but I found him not . . . I charge you, O daughters of Jerusalem, if ye find my beloved, tell him that I am sick of love. . . .' The women's voices lament in the background. Soon the viola is playing a new melody, more hopeful, rising. Suddenly, distant, and then, immediately, nearer, a march tune is announced: 'Behold his bed, which is Solomon's. Threescore valiant men are about it. . . . They all hold swords, being expert in war', a march which at the outset resembles the march theme from the last movement of the 'London' Symphony. The consecutive fourths of the woodwind and the accompanying cymbals give it an oriental colour so unmistakable that I have, to my horror, heard the accusation that this episode could have come out of 'Chu Chin Chow'. I banish the unworthy thought, but I must confess that 'Flos Campi' comes to me — and I rarely see pictures in music —

as a series of jewel-coloured Persian miniatures. This movement suggests the arriving cortège of some Eastern princess — the kind of picture painted in music by many a Russian composer. The viola plays a more streamlined melody over the martial rhythm. The march is taken up louder and louder by the various instruments and the men's voices. The soloist takes up the tune also, the player attacking his viola with alarming determination. The choir bursts, wordlessly, into ecstasy: 'Return, return, O Shulamite!' reads the quotation, 'Return, return, that we may look upon thee. ... How beautiful are thy feet with shoes, O Prince's daughter.' The viola continues to rhapsodise with abandon, playing some passages in chords of almost nineteenth-century luxuriance. Drumbeats keep up the excitement. When, eventually, the music dies down, over a beat from the tabor, a quiet diatonic tune, charged with peace, takes over, altering the whole character of the music: 'set me as a seal upon thine heart.' We have been led up through this strange, original texture of sound into a world that was to become familiar to Vaughan Williams's listeners in the years that followed, through 'Job', the D major Symphony and 'The Pilgrim's Progress', and to which the 'Pastoral' Symphony before had been the gateway. This ecstatic last movement makes its gradual descent to the inevitable 'niente', while across it, as if to emphasise the difference from the indeterminate polytonality of the first movement and the sure triumphant harmony of the last, various instruments run, quite simply, up and up the major scale. Before the end is reached there is an interruption. Oboe and viola play again their plaintive opening notes. The peaceful song is resumed, the viola breathing it like a sigh. The last movement, in its celestial peace, suggests perhaps that to choose one interpretation of the 'Song of Solomon' or another may be too great a simplification. But interpret it as we will, 'Flos Campi' stands as music pure and simple — music as original and personal as any Vaughan Williams has conceived; not only the precious ornament of modern English music, but of European art as a whole.

'Flos Campi', though it dates from that period of the composer's development when he was removing himself further and

further away from the ordinary musical public and into his unknown region, has managed to win for itself a degree of popularity. With the F minor Symphony, the climax of the twelve
years covered by this chapter, it secures for itself a reasonable
number of performances in the course of the years. 'Sancta
Civitas', his first and, to date, his only oratorio, is heard less often.
In this time of searching and discovery, this post-war flight away
from bluff down-to-earth Englishness towards the thoughts inspired by the Mass, the mystical poets, the Song of Solomon and
now the Revelation of St. John the Divine, Vaughan Williams
progressed so far as to be, in the words of an essay by Basil Maine,
'temporarily out of sight.' Maine was writing, principally, about
the symphony that followed ten years later. Looking back on the
writings of the music critics in those years, I believe that the
furthest withdrawal Vaughan Williams ever made from his audiences turns out to be, not that symphony after all, but this white,
intense, and, at the same time, curiously unassuming re-creation of
the vision of St. John on Patmos. Frank Howes, whose devotion
to and understanding of his music is unquestioned, wrote in 1937
'I still stick at "Sancta Civitas". Everyone I have ever met who
has sung in the work likes it; but almost everyone I have asked
who knows it only as a listener reports that he cannot get on with
it.' In 1953 Percy Young was still able to write ' "Sancta Civitas"
will never attain popularity.'

I have never heard this oratorio properly and I ought not, I
suppose, to venture to include it in this book. Most of the performances, in the years I have been searching for it, were in places
like Rome and Buffalo, U.S.A., though the Three Choirs Festival
and the Leeds Festival have performed it. It has been heard in Aus-
tralia but does not seem to find its way to London. Some years ago
I heard it broadcast from a Region, accompanied by curious crack-
lings and fadings that were not, I think, intended in the score. It
was in the early days of my enthusiasm and, like Frank Howes, I
'stuck' at it. This did not make me downhearted, because by then
I had learned that the first time I heard it I heartily disliked much
of what afterwards became my favourite music. In the years that

followed I searched the papers and the posters in vain for an announcement of a concert performance, and no single opportunity to hear the work properly has ever come my way. The B.B.C. did broadcast it on the composer's eightieth birthday, maddeningly timing the performance to coincide with the special celebration concert which was given at the Festival Hall. I had to choose between the rare work and the compelling necessity to be in that place at that time to add to the enthusiasm. But 'Sancta Civitas' cannot be left out, for its importance in this chapter of Vaughan Williams's development, and in the whole design of his life's music, is vital. It is unlike any other work he has ever written (of how many of his works one could say that!) but it follows logically on the music that comes before it. It is not a surprise coming from Vaughan Williams's pen in the early fifties of his life; but it is an astonishing work to find appearing from any source in the middle 'twenties of this century. Vaughan Williams wrote in his essay on Beethoven 'a composer is most truly himself and at his greatest when he is least his superficial self, when he casts off all the trappings of his technique and period and enables his thought to stand out in all its nakedness'. By this criterion 'Sancta Civitas' is among his greatest works; it is the first of a succession of peaks, standing, with 'Job' and the succeeding symphonies, above and apart from the more comfortable, more easily accessible music that is more generally popular and more constantly performed.

I was rescued from the predicament of having altogether to omit this important work by a recording made in the United States — a country where records of English works are sometimes made before our own recording companies have even heard of them. It is an incomplete performance for there is no orchestra, but only an organ for accompaniment. With the help of a vocal score that indicates some of the orchestration I have tried to arrive, in my imagination, at something near an understanding of what this music should really sound like. On that unsatisfactory basis only can I attempt to fill this gap.

A quotation in Greek from the *Phaedo* of Plato prefaces the score. The discourse has been on the immortality of the soul and the passage states that though no man may know the truth about this matter, he may worthily and properly venture to believe in it, for the venture is noble, and he does well to let the music of such beliefs steal upon his spirits.

'Sancta Civitas' (The Holy City) was published in 1925 and first performed in Oxford in the following year. It is built up in three tiers, progressively more remote; chorus and orchestra with a baritone soloist; above them a semi-chorus of about twenty singers, and higher still, invisible indeed, if circumstances permit, a distant choir of voices that should, if possible, belong to boys. Hidden with the choir is a trumpet that plays a two-note fanfare of a rising fifth each time the invisible singers are to be heard. The effect is architectural, or like a religious painting in which the denizens of earth and heaven are seen simultaneously in rising layers. It is perhaps this element of space and perspective between the parts of the chorus that continually, in this work, recalls Holst's music to the mind; and Holst is recalled also by a combination of fire and ice that is like the 'Hymn of Jesus' in feeling, though the actual music is as little like Holst's as any ever written by Vaughan Williams. We go to Vaughan Williams instinctively for warmth. Even the deliberate pictorial coldness he creates in the 'Sinfonia Antartica' is warm beside the remote and other-worldly music that seems to come from infinitely high above us in 'Sancta Civitas'. This rarefied atmosphere, the sharp jewel-hard dissonances that illustrate the glories of the Holy City, more than account for the unwillingness of 1926 to take the music to its heart. There is, moreover, about the quieter passages in this work, an austerity, a deliberate shunning of all sensuous beauty of sound for its own sake, a plainness, an impersonality, which are moving today but may well have been forbidding to the original audiences. In almost all Vaughan Williams's writing for the voice the words lead the music, and in this work, more than in any other but its near neighbour 'Riders to the Sea', this is true. The white-hot climaxes at the topmost possible pitch of all the voices seem to be dragged out of the composer by the compulsion of the text. There is no straining whatever for dramatic effect. Even the direction to the conductor on the first page of the score bears this out — 'The tempo marks are approximate. The pace must be free and elastic throughout'.

The oratorio is in the form of a triptych — three contrasted pictures that make a unity — but there is no break in the music between the sections. The first is of the blesssed in heaven praising God with Alleluias, from the 19th chapter of the Revelation, and includes the terrifying vision of the white horse and his rider whose name was 'Faithful and True'. The middle section, which comes from the previous chapter, is a lament over the fall of Babylon. The third is a description of the Holy City, taken from the 21st and 22nd chapters with the addition of the Sanctus from the Communion service.

The music emerges out of silence, beginning with a deep muttering from the 'cellos and basses and a succession of mysterious alternating chords a major second apart, and vanishes again at the end into silence by the way it came. The baritone soloist softly intones 'I was in the spirit and I heard a voice as of much people praising God and saying Alleluia' and before he has finished the semi-chorus and the full chorus have taken up the word, repeating it quietly. The distant trumpet with its two notes announces the unseen choir singing in consecutive fifths 'Alleluia, salvation and glory, honour and power unto the Lord our God'. The Alleluias continue, mounting, until, almost imperceptibly, we arrive at the first terrific climax of the work — 'For the Lord God omnipotent reigneth' in which the sopranos must reach high B. The vision passes to the 'marriage supper of the Lamb' and his bride in 'fine linen clean and white', and then to a short orchestral passage which returns us to the opening bars of the work. This is the introduction for the description of the white horse and his rider. The baritone sings 'And I saw Heaven opened' and both choruses unite to sing with gathering ferocity until, by the time they reach the words 'and he treadeth the winepress of the fierceness and wrath of Almighty God', the music has attained a savage fortissimo hardly equalled even in the F minor Symphony.

The brutal force with which Vaughan Williams depicts this 'King of Kings and Lord of Lords' in his interpretation of the Revelation knows no compromise. The passage that follows is sung in unison by the full chorus — 'I saw an angel standing in the sun — ', and it culminates in yet another terrible climax on the word 'slain', sung to a descending five note scale of hideous fury. The baritone finishes the episode singing 'and all the fowls were filled with their flesh.'

The second picture, the lament for Babylon, is sensuously beautiful by contrast. The women of the semi-chorus set its atmosphere in a falling phrase like a great sigh — 'Babylon the great is fallen, is fallen' — four times repeated in the course of the episode. The full chorus lament 'Alas, alas', and the voices of each part add their separate lamentation. But the distant choir is pitiless. In their original bright key, announced by their trumpet, they cry 'Rejoice over her, O heavens, for God hath aveng'd you on her.' The baritone tells of the mighty angel who cast a millstone into the sea saying 'Thus with violence shall that great city Babylon be thrown down.' The lament is resumed and the final repetition of the beautiful pattern — 'Babylon the great is fallen' — leads to a quiet valediction by the cor anglais.

Up till this moment Vaughan Williams has shown himself as impersonal as in any music that he had ever written, and that in spite of as many consecutive triads and fifths and as much 'false relation' as any work could contain. Now the violin, that instrument he called his 'musical salvation', ascends out of the depths to spin an upward-soaring arabesque of melody that is suddenly familiar, warm and reassuring — its voice, mellowed from the solo part in 'The Lark Ascending', foreshadows an episode in 'Job'. 'And I saw a new heaven and a new earth; for the first earth and the first heaven were passed away; and there was no more sea.' The vision comes pianissimo, gently, 'as a bride adorned for her husband', almost sadly. It is not unnatural for the composer whose last full-scale choral work was a 'Sea' Symphony to set the words 'and there was no more sea' to a phrase of infinite regret. The oboe takes over from the violin to lift its descant over the still hushed voices of the semi-chorus as they describe the light which was 'like unto a stone most precious, even like a jasper stone, clear as crystal,' but the violin is back once more as they tell of the twelve gates that were twelve pearls. When the men of the chorus relate 'I saw no temple therein, for the Lord God Almighty is the temple of it' there comes another striking presage of 'Job', and also of 'Hodie', more than twenty years later, The strings descend a sweeping majestic scale, and this phrase, modified, became in Vaughan Williams's music a constant symbol of the majesty of God. When the description of the city is over and the violin has descended from the heights above to the depths from which it came, the distant trumpet is heard again and the unseen choir begin the Sanctus — 'Holy, holy, holy; Lord God Almighty'. The full chorus and semi-chorus take up the words of the Communion and continue in counterpoint, growing more and more remote and other-worldly.

Finally, after a pause, and the two chords of the opening repeated, a solo tenor, reserved for this moment, this one high clear call, cries — 'Behold I come quickly. I am the bright and the morning star. Surely I come quickly'. The chorus, half speaking, mutter under their breath — 'Amen, even so come, Lord'. The vision fades mysteriously and slowly into the silence out of which it came.

I do not think that Percy Young is right. I believe that, thirty years late, 'Sancta Civitas' might achieve popularity. A performance now would find a large and expectant audience. For myself, my American record that gives me a faint glimmer of what must be the white unsparing radiance of this music has stirred me to vast impatience. I long to hear it in all its glory.

The time had come for Vaughan Williams to turn his attention to music for the stage. In the year of the 'Pastoral' Symphony he had composed a one-act opera for six singers, chorus and chamber orchestra, 'The Shepherds of the Delectable Mountains', which seems to have been the beginning of his thirty years' dalliance with 'The Pilgrim's Progress'. I am going to leave this work out of the discussion, however, until we reach 1951, when it had been incorporated as one scene into 'The Pilgrim's Progress' opera, Vaughan Williams's contribution to the Festival of Britain at Covent Garden.

Writing operas seems to give Vaughan Williams particular pleasure, and it is sad that his efforts in this sphere have brought him very little success. It is, I think, true to say that only one of his operas is a finished work of art, but one would have thought that, by their tunefulness alone, three of the others should have been enormously popular. In England, however, we have a peculiar attitude to opera.

The first of the operas, 'Hugh the Drover', seems to have been the luckiest. It even was recorded in pre-electrical days, and in a most curiously potted version. With the notable exception of one brief interlude from 'Sir John in Love', and a few songs out of 'The Pilgrim's Progress' thinly accompanied by piano, not a bar from any of the others has attained this distinction.

Vaughan Williams did not have to make a living, a circumstance fortunate for us and for opera alike. He was free to indulge his fancy in writing works for the stage for which, I imagine, he could see no immediate hope of production except by amateurs and students. 'Riders to the Sea', written in 1926, not published until 1937, had no professional performance on the stage until 1953. 'Sir John in Love', written in 1929, was not performed, except by amateurs, until 1946. 'The Poisoned Kiss' has never been professionally performed.

Of course it is entirely typical of our British attitude to the arts that the music promoters of this country should have seized avidly upon all the serious, forbidding, contemplative music Vaughan Williams has composed, and presented it to us often enough to batter the public into acceptance; at the same time rejecting operas which are filled to overflowing with tunes, light romantic music, music that should have greatly assisted the acceptance of his heavier works, and, at the same time, have gone a long way towards dispelling the idea, still prevalent, that 'melody' and 'modern music' are incompatible. The tunes in 'Sir John in Love', like those in 'Hugh the Drover', would echo, long after their performance, in the ears of any audience given the chance to hear them. It is a disaster that so much lovely music should be shut away in books, collecting dust upon a shelf.

Benjamin Britten, with his wonderful opera 'Peter Grimes', broke the evil spell that had been binding English opera for longer than any of us can remember. Since its success English operas have been produced with alarming frequency, though quite half the number are also by Benjamin Britten. Apart from 'Peter Grimes' they do not seem to be able to keep their place in the repertoire. They are given a brief airing for three or four performances at Sadler's Wells, so little advertised that one generally hears about them only to find that they are over; or they are heralded with fanfares and given colossal premières at Covent Garden, where, for the most part, they fall curiously flat and are never performed anywhere again.

'Riders to the Sea' had its first brief airing at Sadler's Wells in the summer of 1953, sharing the evening with the shortened version of 'Hugh the Drover', an arrangement pleasing to those who enjoy both the tuneful and the discordant Vaughan Williams, the traditionalist and the pioneer. 'Riders to the Sea' has no claim at all to the adjective 'tuneful'. My first acquaintance with this short opera — it lasts about thirty-five minutes —was in a broadcast, at a time when I was just becoming familiar with the composer's most popular and characteristic works. Its effect upon me, though I carried not one note of it away in my head, was only a little less staggering than the effect of the F minor Symphony. I was convinced against all the evidence — infrequency of performance, tepid reaction of critics — that this was an overwhelming masterpiece. It is a triumph, moreover, brought off against great odds. Vaughan Williams's aim in this short opera was not to produce attractive music, but, letting the music wait upon the words, so to follow the inflections of speech heightened by drama, as to produce the perfect translation of Synge's prose-poetry into musical sound and rhythm, as from one language into another. It is the method used by Debussy in 'Pelléas et Mélisande', and it is a method that Vaughan Williams uses sometimes in his songs; in the haunting, lissom lines of 'The New Ghost', to words by Frede-gond Shove, for instance, which dated from the year of the 'Pastoral' Symphony.

The choice of the Synge play is surprising. Vaughan Williams's choice of literature for setting to music follows, on the whole, a predictable pattern; the Bible, Bunyan, the mystical poets, and, among secular writers, Shakespeare and Skelton, Housman and Whitman. The dreary, miserable story of the Irish peasant woman Maurya, and of how the sea claimed each of her six sons, the musical, Irish inflection of Synge's prose, the bleak atmosphere of the poor cottage on the rocky Galway coast are as foreign to Vaughan Williams's mind as anything the English language could produce. But the choice was a stroke of genius. 'Riders to the Sea' is constructed in such a way as to provide a perfect libretto for a composer who does not insist on anything in the nature of formal arias and set pieces. It is a gradual building up of tension and drama in which, from the composer's point of view, there is hardly a superfluous word or action. Even such mechanical details as the blowing open of the cottage door can be turned to musical effect.

I hated this dreary little play when I saw it on the stage of the Abbey Theatre in Dublin and it took Vaughan Williams's illum-ination of the text to convince me of its greatness. Miserable and sordid stories, for some inscrutable reason, often make the basis of moving and exciting opera. The stories of 'Wozzek' and of 'Peter Grimes', for example, could hardly be more desolate and sordid, and what magnificent operas they make.

'Riders to the Sea' tells the story of how Maurya, who has lost her husband and four of her sons to the sea, whose fifth son Michael has been missing a week on a journey, quarrels with Bartley, the one remaining son, because he insists on taking horses to the mainland on a stormy evening. He leaves the cottage with her curses in his ears. Nora and Kathleen, Maurya's daughters, per-suade her to go down to the quayside to make her peace with him and give him a loaf of bread. She comes back having seen him rid-ing to the sea, followed by his missing brother, in fine clothes, on the grey pony. This vision shows her that both are lost. The grey pony knocks Bartley into the waves and he is drowned. Peasants carry his body home and fill the cottage with their keening. But Maurya is triumphant, the sea has done all it can to her, and she can rest.

The form of the opera, not unlike that of 'Flos Campi', is a progression; from stormy daylight to darkness on the stage; from muttering disquiet, through sustained visionary incantation, to broad arioso in a major key over a sustained accompaniment, in the music. The translation of text and action into music is so skilfully managed that, watching it on the stage, I have found myself forgetting that it is opera or music at all; and this I presume to be the composer's intention. The strained, hushed voices of the girls, with only an occasional chord from the orchestra to support them, seem to be speaking in the most natural accents possible; when the door blows open a wind machine reinforces a theme in the orchestra that, throughout the action, represents the menacing sea. The orchestra is a small one; the brass limited to a trumpet and two horns. It is not until the return of the old woman and the recital of her vision — 'I seen the fearfullest thing!' — that the music forces itself on the attention with claims of its own, and the passage where she tells of the fate of her other sons, with her daughters keening in the background, is hair-raising and musically very beautiful. There begins here a slow preparation for the final calm arioso passages, when, after the body of Bartley has been brought home, the women all kneeling about it, Maurya sings 'They are all gone now, and there isn't anything more the sea can do to me' to a broad melody of great beauty, rising into the major for 'But it's a great rest I'll have now, and it's time surely — '. The scene fades into darkness and silence, the wind lingering longest, as Maurya utters her prayer for all the dead, while her daughters, in undertones, tell each other 'She's getting old now, and broken'.

For many people 'Riders to the Sea' will hardly exist as opera. Opera, for most people, still means arias, prima donnas, colour and glamour, none of which are to be found in this score; but I think Vaughan Williams, in submitting himself to the rigid discipline of J. M. Synge's text, has produced here far greater music than is to be found in any of his more conventionally operatic works. The strange beauty of this score, as unique in its way as 'Flos Campi', was perfectly reflected in Clive Carey's production at Sadler's Wells, the most flawless production I have seen of any opera.

'Sir John in Love' is as unlike 'Riders to the Sea' as one opera possibly could be to another. Why it is not constantly performed upon the stage is one of those mysteries that will never be solved. Here is an opera that has romance, comedy, action, words set so that they are as audible as if the play was performed without music; and, added to these qualities, a score as tuneful as any by Sullivan, but with tunes that are sweeter, fresher, more spontaneous, more lovingly clothed in rich tissues of orchestral colour than anything Sullivan could ever compose. The place for this is not, I am convinced, an opera house at all. It should be put on for a run in a smallish West End theatre, advertised as a comedy with music, where, I am quite convinced, it would remain for months and months.

The performance of this opera at Sadler's Wells in 1946 failed, for some unfathomable reason, to convince the audience of the opera's worth at all. It was a tame and disappointing occasion, though how any producer or singers could fail to be inspired by the tremendous vitality of the music I cannot imagine. So I did not discover the ravishing delights of 'Sir John in Love', except through some broadcasts in the Third Programme (not its natural home), until I saw the Cambridge University Opera Group perform it at the Arts Theatre in the chilly spring of 1956. They may not have been trained singers, their costumes (old Stratford-upon-Avon pattern) contrasted strangely with their settings (nineteen-twenties cubist), but somebody, or perhaps everybody, knew what the opera was about and put it over with rude enjoyment and reckless vigour. Some of the dons had, so one of them confessed to me, been listening to a performance of Verdi's 'Falstaff' the previous week, and went into the Arts with nervous half-apologetic looks. By the first interval they were visibly unbending; at the end they left the theatre purring with satisfaction.

Before examining the score of 'Sir John — ' it is instructive to have a look at the preface the composer wrote for it. This much-quoted passage is unusually long for Vaughan Williams and quite extraordinarily apologetic. He would seem to be suffering from a 'guilt complex' for having dared to borrow Falstaff for his own purposes, though the subject is clearly one that would attract him. Hubert Foss, indeed, suggests that 'Falstaff had been slyly standing at Vaughan Williams's elbow for many long years'. The composer excuses himself, more or less, from the necessity of apologising to Shakespeare, on the reasonable grounds that he is 'fair game, like the Bible, and may be made use of . . . even for advertisements for soap and razors'. He dares to hope that 'Even Verdi's masterpiece does not exhaust the possibilities of Shakespeare's genius' and apologises to Holst for imitating his use of folk-song in connection with this subject as Holst had done in his one-act opera 'At the Boar's Head'. 'My chief object in "Sir John in Love",' he writes, 'is to fit this wonderful comedy with, I trust, not unpleasant music. In the matter of the folk-tunes, they appear only occasionally and their titles have no dramatic relevancy (except possibly in the case of "John, come kiss me now"). When a particular folk-song appeared to be the fitting accompaniment to the situation, I have used it. When I could not find a suitable folk-tune, I have made shift to make up something of my own. I therefore offer no apology for the occasional use of folk-song to enhance a dramatic point. If the result is successful I feel justified; if not, no amount of "originality" will save the situation. However, the point is a small one, since out of a total of 120 minutes of music the folk-tunes occupy less than 15.' The point may have *been* a small one, but the passage has been quoted so often in connection with Vaughan Williams's use of folk-song in general that I should imagine he must be heartily sorry he ever wrote it.

Not everyone can entirely agree with his estimate of the play, 'this wonderful comedy,' as he calls it; but perhaps he saw it always, instinctively, as opera. After seeing it as opera I doubt if anyone would be satisfied with a *Merry Wives* without music ever again. 'The text', Vaughan Williams continues, 'is taken

G   R.V.W.

almost entirely from *The Merry Wives*, with the addition of lyrics from Elizabethan poets. A few unimportant remarks (e.g. "Here comes Master Ford") are my own.' He has vastly improved the quality of his chosen play by these pilferings among the other Elizabethans, and from Shakespeare's other plays. 'Sigh no more ladies' is imported from *Much Ado* — ; 'When daisies pied — ' is dragged in from *Love's Labour's Lost*. He borrows enthusiastically from Thomas Middleton, Ben Jonson and one John Still, Bishop of Bath and Wells. The difference between the finished libretto of 'Sir John in Love' and *The Merry Wives* is that Vaughan Williams's play is sweeter and more romantic than Shakespeare's. Both by the importation of lyrics from other sources and also by the radiance of the love music, he has tilted the balance of interest a little away from Falstaff and towards Anne Page and her lover Fenton. The music with which he has fitted this comedy is really 'not unpleasant' in the very least; neither the much-debated folk-songs, nor the 105 minutes of music he had to 'make shift' to make up of his own. His 'chief object' was triumphantly achieved.

'John, come kiss me now' is an aptly-chosen signature tune for the fat knight, but, on the whole, the folk-tunes do not get the best of it, though, without the footnotes in the score for guide, it would be impossible for anyone but an expert to disentangle these fifteen minutes from the surrounding opera. What would one decide at a guess about the origin of 'Back and side go bare — ' for instance, a glorious drinking song by Vaughan Williams that could easily have been sung somewhere around the streets of Southwark by Shakespeare and his actors, rolling home after a successful evening in the theatre? But the Globe audiences would have been astonished at what our twentieth-century composer makes of 'Sigh no more, ladies', a song which is infinitely more appropriate in this situation than in its original context. He invents for it a delicious waltz tune with a hiccup in the accompaniment, which Mistress Quickly sings, with comments from both the affronted 'wives'. Anne Page, from her first entrance, with the haunting little phrases on the oboe, and her song 'Weep eyes, break heart, My love and I must part', to the rapturous chorus for her wedding which is the climax of the last act, is followed by music so gently lovely that it would be hard indeed to find a singer to live up to its sweet descriptiveness. It is in the first scene that her suitor, Fenton, begins to prepare us for that great chorus, singing a verse of Jonson's poem:

> Have you seen but a bright lily grow
> Before rude hands have touched it?
> Have you marked but the fall of the snow
> Before the soil has smutched it?
> Have you felt the wool of the beaver,
> Or swan's down ever?
> Or have smelt o' the bud of the briar,
> Or the nard in the fire?
> Or have tasted the bag of the bee?
> O so white, O so soft, O so sweet is she!

in a setting that is unexpectedly rich and romantic for such thistle-down verse. This song gives to Fenton a character rounder and fuller than Shakespeare seems to have allowed him, and Vaughan Williams has made, in this way, several of the well-known personages of the play grow to a sharper life; Sir Hugh Evans with his Welsh accent and his book of Psalms — 'When as we sat in Papylon — '; the angry Dr Caius melting suddenly into the old French melody 'Vrai dieu d'amour, confortez moy — ', and the jealous Ford with his tender song of reconciliation 'Pardon me, wife — ' become so much more real in this score as to take a little of the limelight away from the central figure of Falstaff.

'Why does it sound familiar?' asks Frank Howes in his analysis, published in the *Musical Pilgrim* in 1937, about the orchestral prelude to this song by Ford. He answers his own question convincingly enough. But no, the answer will not do for me; or only partly. Coming, as I did, to all Vaughan Williams's music in the wrong order, this lovely, warm and kindly music — so much too little of it, both of prelude and of song — sounded familiar because it recalled the Symphony in D and other music written years later than 'Sir John in Love'. The loving-kindness expressed in this music — 'andante piacevole' — forgiving and blessing, hauntingly foreshadows later music in an atmosphere that is, for the moment, completely un-Shakespearian.

A few years after the publication of 'Sir John in Love' the composer added to it a Prologue, an Episode and an Interlude. The Interlude, which is an expansion of Anne Page's romance, contains a lovely song for Fenton — 'Beauty clear and fair' — to words by John Fletcher. For this song alone the Interlude is indispensable; but the chorus that follows it, to a waltz tune, 'Fair and fair and twice so fair — ' is an uncommonly polite and tame melody for Vaughan Williams, and helps me to understand, for a moment, what people mean when they protest a dislike of folk-song.

Up till the last scene, which takes place beneath the blasted oak in Windsor Forest, where Sir John waits for his assignations with the 'wives', the pace of the opera has been a comfortable amble, reflecting the leisurely life of the people of Windsor as Shakespeare has portrayed it in this, his most domestic play —a little drinking, a bit of love-making, an intrigue or two to pass the time. But in the last scene, in which all the strands of the plot are unravelled simultaneously, the action and the music wake up to a considerable pitch of excitement. The darkened stage is invaded by a host of imitation fairies, who encircle Falstaff, dancing in an insistent teasing rhythm as they pinch him, torment him, and singe him with their tapers. The whole of Windsor seems to turn out to witness the fun. In the general melée Anne Page's two suitors, Slender and Dr Caius, discover that they have been tricked into 'marrying' two small boys, and Anne herself slips away to her true love. At the height of the bewilderment occasioned by these discoveries a harp arpeggio strikes on the midnight air and a distant chorus begin the ravishing strains of Jonson's:

> *See the chariot at hand here of love*
> *Wherein my lady rideth,*

the same song that Fenton had begun in the first act. It modulates, for the second verse, into the dark key of F minor in a manner that fairly makes the heart turn over.

The opera ends with everybody reconciled and happy. Falstaff, joined presently by the other characters of the plot, and eventually by the full chorus, rounds off the play with words taken from Rosseter's *Book of Airs*:

> *Whether men do laugh or weep,*
> *Whether they do wake or sleep,*
> *Whether they die young or old,*
> *Whether they feel heat or cold,*
> *There is underneath the sun*
> *Nothing in true earnest done.*

But this is not quite the end, for the whole company break into a folk-dance, 'Half Hannikin', bringing the opera to a conclusion with the statement:

> *All the world is but a play.*

I must not leave 'Sir John in Love' without a brief reference to a very curious matter. There was a crusty moralist called Philip Stubbs who, living in the days of Queen Elizabeth, nevertheless found nothing pleasant or admirable in any aspect of English life at all. He railed against everything and everybody, from the immorality of the clergy to the thickness of the soles of women's shoes. A tune called 'Greensleeves' came in for his especial condemnation, a 'plaguey' tune which was whistled by every errand boy in the street until Mr Stubbs was forced to plug his ears. I thought Mr Stubbs made an absurd fuss about so small a matter and so nice a tune until, some time during the war (I think) the recording companies, the B.B.C., the public, and, once again, the errand boys, began the trouble all over again. Vaughan Williams's 'Fantasia on Greensleeves', lifted bodily out of its appropriate context as an interlude in 'Sir John — ', with an arrangement of the bawdy song 'Lovely Joan' set in the middle of it, probably earned him more money than anything of his own he has composed. I do not suppose that any other tune has ever achieved the distinction of driving people mad in two separate centuries, and I have no doubt that more people know of Vaughan Williams as the 'composer' of 'that pretty tune "Greensleeves"' than know him for any other or better reason.

I find the word 'romantic' has crept into these pages rather often; but always as an adjective describing music that concerns young love. I have never precisely understood the meaning of the word when it is applied wholesale to a composer, unless, of course, he belongs to that period of musical history that is normally covered by that heading. In his autobiography, *Farewell my Youth*, the late Sir Arnold Bax claims the title 'Romantic' for himself because of his preoccupation with the irrecoverable past. Delius is the most obviously 'romantic' of twentieth-century composers, his music being concerned, almost exclusively, with the translation into sound of a nostalgia for lost youth and fading beauty. There is not a trace of this beautiful regret in the music of Vaughan Williams, except perhaps in Aunt Jane's sad song, 'Life must be full of care — ' from 'Hugh the Drover', which is probably, now I come to think of it, why I have always felt this pleasant tune to be quite untypical of its composer. Despite his historical interests Vaughan Williams's music lives in the present. Growing older, he quickly shook off the faint mist of youthful melancholy that hung about the early song-cycles. He has grown more and more positive with age, almost as if he welcomed the advancing years. His investigations of the music of the past have not been those of the antiquarian or the lover of the past at the expense of the present. His purpose was utilitarian; to discover stirring songs to replace the sentimental Victorian horrors of much of *A & M* and add a new vigour to our church services; to enrich the repertoire of the cathedral choir; to establish a solid basis of English melody on which our composers could build, free from the German tradition that had stifled English music from the days of Handel until he and his contemporaries arose to liberate it. It took a short acquaintance only with his music to send me to the list of his compositions in *Grove* in search of a setting of the 'Benedicite'. I had no doubt that I should find one. Worship and praise, with contemplation of an unregretful nature, are the principal exercises of his mind, no matter to what objects they are directed. The magnificent procession of praises in this canticle must have been irresistible. I can conceive of nothing more apt for his inspiration.

The 'Benedicite' was written in 1930, for the twenty-fifth birthday of the Leith Hill Music Festival, which Vaughan Williams had founded and had conducted all those years. He has divided the canticle into four parts; the first elemental, 'O all ye works of the Lord, bless ye the Lord'; the second pastoral, 'O let the Earth bless the Lord'; a short poem by the seventeenth-century poet John Austin makes the third section; the finale is a recapitulation of all the blessing and praise. The opening is terrific; stern and virile and extremely Protestant. The unadorned praise theme strides through the brass and is shouted out by the chorus. The piano, used so seldom by Vaughan Williams in its accustomed character, comes in here, as in many of his later works, as an instrument of percussion; cymbal clashes give colour. This is about as unmellifluous as modern music can be, but I doubt if it could ever give rise to that pathetic cry so often heard from those who cling lovingly to the belief that modern music is incomprehensible — 'I don't know what the music is about!' It is only too plain, and as invigorating as a hail-storm. The soprano, led in by the pastoral tones of the oboe, introduces the theme of Earth. Her voice lifts itself above the chorus and sinks back in continuous curves. The brass is silent. There are passages where the chorus sings unaccompanied, moving in dignified parallel chords. The oboe returns from time to time and the drum recalls the opening phrases in a persistent rhythm. The celesta doubles the voice parts, its faintly exotic tones unexpected in this astringent context. John Austin's three-verse poem is introduced by the soprano while the chorus sing 'praise Him and magnify Him' under and through her melody:

> *Hark, my soul, how everything*
> *Strives to serve our bounteous King.*

The end:

> *Live for ever, Glorious Lord,*
> *Live by all thy works adored,*
> *One in three and three in one,*
> *Thrice we bow to thee alone.*

works up to a finale in which the full weight of the orchestra returns to reaffirm, with the chorus, the stirring praises of the opening.

Unquestionably the most magnificent music ever written specially for the ballet is Vaughan Williams's 'Job'. It has been objected that it is not really a ballet at all, and the composer himself, disliking the word in this connection, subtitled it 'A Masque for Dancing'. To appreciate it fully it is necessary both to see it in action on the stage and to hear it in concert performance. Without illustration by dancing some of the precise meaning of the music is lost — the sweeping descending phrase as God tells Satan, 'Lo, all that he hath is in thy power,' and the hypocritical comforters, whose sickly saxophone tune in woeful jazz rhythm can hardly make its point if the listener has not read the quotation over that part of the score. On the other hand, the music is far too great to be tied for ever to a stage production that is bound to focus more than half one's attention. Music for the ballet really has no business to be as overwhelming on its own account as this score is. 'Job', however, as a concert suite appears quite often in programmes.

The inspiration for this work was twofold: the Book of Job and the illustrations for it by William Blake, and one cannot praise the music more highly than to say that it amply holds its own beside those works of art. But it is a work of art in its own right, owing nothing but its inspiration to the past and its downright certainty and tremendous virtuosity are almost intimidating. Never before was Vaughan Williams so sure of himself — or that is the impression that the music gives. The facts may have been quite otherwise, for he tells the story, in his chapter of autobiography, of how Gustav Holst almost had to go down on his knees to him at rehearsal to implore him to cut out at least half of the percussion. Some of the music is celestially beautiful, some of it is harsh, ugly and horrifying, some of it has a gentle pastoral flow; but only once is it friendly, in the manner to which his earlier works had accustomed us, when 'The Lark Ascending' is unexpectedly recalled after long scenes of violence and horror.

Just as there are three scenes of action on the stage — Heaven,

Earth and Hell — so there are three kinds of music in 'Job'.
Heaven's music is simple, majestic, wide-intervalled and diatonic,
with formal seventeenth-century dance rhythms; Earth has music
that is pastoral, with smaller intervals and a flowing measure; the
music of Hell is chromatic and discordant, with jagged rhythms and
oddly-placed emphasis. Heaven opens to disclose the Sons of God
revolving round His throne to a stately Sarabande. It is with seem-
ingly unquestioning confidence that Vaughan Williams evolves
this tune, and the sublime Pavane and Galliard of the Sons of the
Morning later in the ballet, rolling back the clouds to discover for
us the courteous dance in all its expected dignity, both childlike
and strong, the absolute translation of Blake into sound. There is
scarcely an accidental in the music of Heaven. When tunes so
inevitable and strong and gracious can be found out from the
eight notes of the mode it seems strange that composers so rarely
place themselves under its discipline. On the Earth the music has a
different character. When Satan strikes dead the sons of Job and their
wives they are dancing to a minuet — but a minuet very different
in mood from the polite formal measure of that name. The composer directs that the dancing should be 'voluptuous' and the
music is as sensuous as anything he has written. It has that odd suggestion of the East that is present in 'Flos Campi', odd, because
again, except for the soft clash of cymbals, he makes no apparent
use of any of the accepted easy means to achieve this atmosphere.
The most impressive episode from the ballet as seen on the stage
is Satan's dance — a tremendous 'aria' for a male dancer. The
music, though it cannot compete for strength with the positive
music of Heaven, is tremendous in its own way — a way new to
Vaughan Williams — percussive, angular, harmonically nerve-
shattering. This was, I suppose, the first occasion when he astonished his hearers with his capacity for making a louder noise
than other composers — to challenge Stravinsky at his own game.
The contrasts in style within 'Job' are remarkable, but they are
dictated by their dramatic relevance and blend into a perfectly
integrated whole. There are, besides, two episodes in two quite
separate styles that fit, without incongruity, at any rate for a stage

performance: the music for Job's comforters and 'Elihu's Dance
of Youth and Beauty'. The comforters are hypocrites, their con-
dolences false comfort, and to symbolise hypocrisy and falseness
Vaughan Williams calls to aid the saxophone. The tune it plays is
in a doleful and half-hearted jazz rhythm. The justification of this
piece of 'impertinence' in the middle of so majestic a score is complete in stage performance, but I have never felt entirely happy
about its effect in the concert hall. For Elihu's dance, a tranquil
passage after the music of Hell and hypocrisy, Vaughan Williams's
familiar solo violin weaves threads of melody 'senza misura' in
calm and happy contemplation, the cold ecstasy of 'The Lark
Ascending' mellowed into warmer gold. It holds a lingering contentment, almost as if the composer were unwilling to leave this
pastoral resting-place and arrive at the bursting glory of the
Pavane and Galliard of the Sons of the Morning. At the back of
this great tune, in which the Heavenly Host drive Satan down
from God's Throne, hangs a faint salt tang of the sea shanty, as if,
for Vaughan Williams at least, God was undoubtedly an Englishman. The ballet ends, as it began, with Job surrounded by his
resurrected family, who dance in gentle country rhythm to the
music of the Earth.

It is probably true to say that Vaughan Williams has been as
prolific a composer of 'Gebrauchmusik' as any other English musician of any fame, although I am sure he would not for one instant
subscribe to the doctrines of Hindemith and his followers in the
German school. Hindemith maintained that music ought only to
be written if it could be shown to fulfil a social function or satisfy
a particular utilitarian demand. Under this heading one could
group all Vaughan Williams's editing and composition of hymns
and hymn-books; his folk-dance arrangements; the music he
wrote in later years for film sound tracks and radio programmes,
even, I suppose, such matters as the writing of his Mass in G minor
or the 'Te Deum' for the Coronation of 1937. Of course he has
set the English liturgy to music. Apart from his special Te Deums
there is a plainer setting of the morning service and an Evensong
as well. But the setting of a Magnificat to be sung at Evensong by

a cathedral choir was not to be expected to satisfy his mind. It is his instinctive habit to go straight to the heart of any matter, and this rapturous paean of praise uttered by a young woman at the most wonderful moment of her life is not really best expressed by rows of well-scrubbed choirboys in neatly starched surplices. Vaughan Williams saw the Magnificat from Mary's point of view, and prepared a concert arrangement of the canticle for contralto solo, women's chorus and orchestra, that has not an echo of the Anglican prayer-book in it anywhere. Mary, the contralto, sings her heartfelt praises warmly over and through the chorus, that uses Gabriel's message — 'Hail, Mary' — to weave arabesques around her in parallel chords. A solo flute, hovering sweetly, personifies the dove. The music, as in a later, sweeter, work for contralto and women's chorus — 'The Lament for Philip Sparrow' — is intensely feminine; strange and moving in the idiom of a composer who has less of the feminine in his artistic make-up than musicians usually have. I have never been able to imagine the Virgin Mary as a contralto, any more than even with Bach's persuasion I can accept Jesus as a bass; but the message of this ancient psalm is delivered in this setting with a truth and poignancy that is never achieved, and perhaps ought not to be achieved, in any arrangement intended to be sung in church.

And now we have come to the Symphony in F minor and the point at which I switched on my wireless and discovered English music. I wonder if anybody else has been lured into a frantic pursuit of music in general by that particular work. Musicians would probably shake their heads at the idea and the composer would undoubtedly be shocked. But I cannot help that. I am not going to pretend that I understood what I heard that day, or that it was easy to arrive at an understanding. I do not know that I can claim to understand it now, but only that I know and love it. In this I seem to be unique. It is really not done to love this symphony. It is to incur the disapproval of the critics who admire its structure and speak with enthusiasm about its greatness, but qualify their praises with adjectives like 'savage', 'fierce' and 'bitter', compare it with an 'edifice of steel and concrete' and insist upon dragging in Fascism; of the public who wholeheartedly dismiss it as a hideous row; and of the composer himself, who was heard to mutter as he descended from the conductor's rostrum — 'If that's what they call "modern music" I don't like it.' This talk of Fascism and war is disturbing, because it occurs in the writings of a great many critics, some of whom, like Frank Howes and Hubert Foss, have made a particular study of Vaughan Williams's work; and there must be some truth in their claims, because, in his next work, 'Dona Nobis Pacem', the composer shows his mind to have been troubled by thoughts of war. I am sorry to have my reactions to the F minor Symphony coloured by these considerations, because, for the second time only in the works we have examined, there is no implied subject. Indeed, this is what the composer said when the work was completed, 'Here is a Symphony, occasionally in the key of F minor. Take it or leave it, for that is nearly all I can tell you about it.' A statement wonderfully un-apologetic for Vaughan Williams, characteristically attached to the work people think most in need of apology!

The symphony was first performed in 1935, the year in which the composer received the Order of Merit. Its immense force came as a tremendous surprise alike to his admirers and detractors. Undoubtedly the surprise was less welcome to his admirers, who were probably looking forward to another work full of his usual tranquillity and contemplation. Vaughan Williams's own reluctance to commit himself to any definite opinions betrays, I think, not so much the dislike he seems to protest, as a sort of bewildered and unwilling admiration. It probably shocked him as much as it shocked his hearers, and in much the same way as parts of *King Lear* probably shocked Shakespeare. His way in the past had been to linger; to draw out his themes into strands of wandering melody; to drift into silence. This symphony is taut, compressed, sparing little time for the development of any theme, hurtling towards its fugal epilogue in one impulse that is barely slackened, even in the slow movement. This sudden power and drive had not, of course, been unheralded. The 'Benedicite' and 'Job' are driven onwards by a similar impulse; but in 'Job' the story of the

ballet dictates that the violence of Satan's music must be interrupted continually by passages of a pastoral or rhapsodic character.
'Job's hearers, moreover, probably accepted the crashing discords
in that work merely as the appropriate trimming of the subject
and did not see in them any indication of the way Vaughan
Williams was to go in the future. In 1934, however, he had published a piano concerto which showed the change in his outlook
more clearly. I have to leave this out of the present discussion
because it is practically never played, although in 1946 Vaughan
Williams rescored it for two pianos. I did once manage to hear a
broadcast of this remarkable work, in which the piano (or pianos)
is used for its percussive qualities, but since, at the time, I had
a temperature of 102, the impression of extraordinary beauty with
which it left me ought not entirely to be trusted. Musicians seem
to think highly of this concerto, Hubert Foss even giving it a place
alongside the symphonies, so it is strange that it is never heard.

Sir Henry Wood was a great admirer of the Symphony in F
minor, which, he tells us in his autobiography, he conducted as often
as four times in a season. He said more about its quality in fewer
words than anybody else whose opinions I have read. 'To my
mind,' he said, 'he has beaten these striving-for-originality moderns at their own game, but with far stronger *musical* results.' That
indeed is the core of the matter; and that is why I deplore these
references to war. The music may seem ugly, discordant, bitter,
whatever epithets you may wish to hurl at it, but it is pre-emin-
ently *musical*. It has far less concern with politics or religion than
his Symphony in D (composed during the war which the F minor
is supposed to foreshadow) which sprung from an admitted
mystical and literary source. The Symphony in F minor is simply
concerned with colossal issues of counterpoint and fugue, and the
organic growth of themes. It is music, whether you like it or not,
that is completely symphonic.

It was thanks to that mixed and misused blessing the gramophone, and a magnificent recording, now deleted, under the composer's own baton, that I got to know this symphony. Falling
under its spell at a first hearing did not make the understanding of

it any easier, indeed, when I procured the records of it I was shattered to find that I could neither recognise it nor discover what it was that had, on the first hearing, thrown me into such a transport of delight — but that is a common experience. Finding its sheer noise and the dissonance to which, in those days, I was not accustomed, a barrier between myself and any concentrated attempt to come to terms with it, I decided to subject myself to one movement daily (as background music) while I cleaned the shoes, deliberately not listening in the hope that I would subconsciously get used to the noise — for I was passionately anxious to recapture my original vision. By the fourth day and the fourth movement the shoes were hurled across the room and I was dancing. Who can help dancing to the genial second subject and the exuberant 'oompah' — Dr Vaughan Williams's word, I assure you, not mine — of the bass? Like the composer, I was not sure whether I liked it, but I began to see what he meant. My first 'live' performance revealed in a sudden overwhelming rush the peculiar and urgent beauty of this music — yes, beauty, and without apologies! If there is no beauty in the unity and architectural shapeliness of this symphony, then musical architecture cannot be beautiful on its own account; if the slow movement is condemned as lacking in beauty, then a great deal of Bach must be condemned with it; if the themes of the first and last movements are not beautiful, there must be something the matter with my ears.

The symphony is entirely built up on two little phrases of four notes each. These little 'motifs' — they are not themes in themselves — are the basis upon which all the thematic material of the symphony is constructed and out of which the whole symphony has grown. I had intended that no musical quotations should appear upon these pages, because this is not a book for musicians and nothing is more thwarting than to be out of reach of a piano, as many amateurs of music are bound to be; but I must quote these two four-note 'germs' because they are so important and because it is possible to appreciate their function with the eye alone. They are:

a)   & *b)*

which, as anybody can see, are as near to a horizontal and to a
vertical line as it is possible for any notes to be. These four-note
motifs are never far away at any point in all the four movements.
They are the bones and sinews of the symphony's structure and
they give it a solidity unique in the history of the symphony.

The F minor Symphony opens with crashing discords and the
two four-note figures are introduced at once and echoed promptly
in diminution — for the untechnically-minded, twice as fast —
both the vertical and the horizontal. Out of the storm emerges a
'cantilena' melody for the strings, soaring with long slow sweeps
of the players' bow arms, over an angular and insistent accompaniment of wind chords. The tension of the movement is so great
that the aching beauty of this theme can hardly take a hold upon
the senses. It leads to a hard and martial theme over a marching
bass — almost as familiar a characteristic of Vaughan Williams's
style as it was of Holst's. This, the most stormy and difficult movement of the symphony, has probably been the cause of many
people abandoning the work without giving the other three a
chance. Undoubtedly it was here that those adjectives — 'bitter',
'fierce' and 'furious' were earned. When the 'cantilena' melody
returns its piercing beauty claims recognition at last, and it leads
into a coda that is soft and dark and calm, though it is a calm
still tremulous with the aftermath of anger.

The tension does not slacken in the slow movement either,
because, although the exquisite counterpoint pursues a calm and
steady course, and the cumulative effect of their weaving and
interweaving is hypnotic, Vaughan Williams has supplied another
of his marching basses in level crotchets, not continuously present
but implicit in the background of one's consciousness, a promise
of violence to come. A version of the vertical theme introduces
the movement on trumpet and trombones and at intervals this
figure is thrown across the music, breaking the sinuous chromatic
flow in sudden anguished climaxes. The movement is divided into

two parts by a passage in which the flute plays a sad descending
wisp of a tune — a 'cadence figure' the composer calls it — and
the sections of the music on either side of this episode are made up
of wandering counterpoints for the various instruments over a
plucked and marching bass. The first half is cold and unfriendly
enough, but after the 'cadence figure's interruption the gradual
adding of one instrument to another builds into a tapestried tissue
of sound that glows into incandescence. This glorious polyphony,
which would surely have gained the admiration of the Tudor
masters, takes a firmer hold on the listener's affections with every
hearing. The flute's little tune, drifting into silence, supplies the
material for the movement's coda.

In the Scherzo humour comes into its own, and reasserts itself
from time to time right up to the symphony's Epilogue. It is not
a kindly humour, I am ready to admit, but if the symphony was,
indeed, concerned with the troubles of the nations, at this point
Vaughan Williams seems to rise above despair into a devil-may-
care detachment. The energetic principal theme is taken from the
vertical figure. The horizontal is shouted out by the brass, mocked,
as usual, in diminution, by the woodwinds. There is a secondary
theme of equal masculine assertiveness. The Trio is an amusing
and heavy-footed wide-intervalled caper for the lowest brass, its
grotesque theme echoed high in the rigging, as it were, by the
highest woodwinds — a breath of blown spume out of the 'Sea'
Symphony's scherzo whistles around the corners of the orchestra.
After the usual repetitions, we come to a strange and almost
unbearably tense passage that bridges without a gap Scherzo into
Finale. Over a timpani pedal its menace is terrifying.

But the explosion, when, at last, it breaks, is followed so
quickly by the 'oompah' bass that bitterness is once more purged
away in the emphatic first tune. The second subject, a first cousin
of the impudent 'London' Symphony tune, leaps out of its context with its shocking audacity. Suddenly the hurtling pace
slackens, the music drops without warning into stillness while, in
a passage of dark tranquillity, something very reminiscent of the
coda to the beautiful first movement theme is recalled by strings

alone. This sudden oasis of quiet is Vaughan Williams's sole concession to the composer he used to be and to that composer's admirers. But the musical impulse is too strong and cannot allow of much lingering and the 'oompah' bass is soon back with its irresistible and jovial urgency. The audacious second subject tune seems almost demure at its recapitulation. The symphony ends with a terrific fugal Epilogue that opens with the horizontal motif blared out on trombones and is based on that figure, right and wrong ways up. To this point the music has been heading since those first tremendous bars of the first movement and here all the elements of the four movements find union. The force is incredible. Ultimately those first bars are repeated and the symphony ends on one explosive note that is the most positive antithesis possible of Vaughan Williams's usual beloved 'niente'.

I have heard this symphony on several occasions from a seat behind the orchestra and can testify that the conductors of it do not seem to view it as a matter for deep despondency. It is true that the orchestra, who work unremittingly throughout this closely-written score, troop on to the platform with a dogged determination on their faces, an expression that melts into exhilaration somewhere early in the Scherzo. On the last occasion Sir Adrian Boult was the conductor. He can conjure more excitement out of a Vaughan Williams score than any other living man. From the joy on his face it was evident that the F minor Symphony was not, for him, primarily an essay in bitterness and world politics. At the conclusion he exchanged with the composer, who was sitting in the front row, a look of delight, complicity and, almost, schoolboy satisfaction, before either of them turned to acknowledge the hearty appreciation of the audience.

The Symphony in F minor, whether you like it or not, completely fulfils the Greek demands for art — 'the purging of the emotions' — if not by 'pity and terror', then by something very nearly akin. To submit to this particular purge is to come forth at the end immensely invigorated, stimulated rather than exhausted, and ready for anything except more music. I recommend it as an infallible cure for depression.

H   R.V.W.

CHAPTER V

1936 - 1945

Dona Nobis Pacem : Five Tudor Portraits : Te Deum : Serenade to Music : Dives and Lazarus : Household Music : Symphony in D : Oboe Concerto : Thanksgiving for Victory

I f the Symphony in F minor can have so great an effect upon its hearers what can have been its effect upon its composer, freed from so weighty a burden? That is something we cannot imagine. But the music that Vaughan Williams wrote between that furious Fourth Symphony and the astonishing and unexpected Sixth of 1948 has a new character. It is glowing with warmth and humanity, strong and immensely sustaining, its direct appeal to the heart disarms critical approach. Often I have set about listening to the music composed during this dozen years or so with my ears pricked determinedly to consider the orchestration or to discover the pattern and logic of the tonality, but always, before many bars are over, I have forgotten my intention and succumbed to the embracing comfort of the music. No longer does Vaughan Williams seem to be practising self-discipline for the sake of perfecting his art, nor is he following after modern trends. These works are the products of a style fully matured, a style that had its first unexpected early flowering in the 'Fantasia on a Theme by Thomas Tallis'. For a time after the F minor Symphony it is as if he had been content to rest from his endless questing, composing music that is simply overflowing with warmth and beauty — a strange thing for a great composer to be at between 1935 and 1944, when the E minor Symphony was ('probably') begun. None of the works he wrote between these years have quite the searching strangeness or compelling imaginative power of, for instance, 'Riders to the Sea' or the Mass in G minor, but these works have a solid basis, every note of them loudly proclaiming its composer. He offers us, for the time being, fewer surprises.

In the year that followed the Symphony in F minor Vaughan Williams's list of publications shows three works — 'The Poisoned Kiss', a comic opera with spoken dialogue, and two large and thoroughly full-blooded choral works. 'The Poisoned Kiss', which few of us have had a chance to see or hear, imprisons within its pages the most delectable of all his love music. Here are tunes he obviously delighted to compose, perhaps as an antidote to the symphony which seems, if we can trust his word, to have given him but little pleasure. Yet there was shame mingled with this delight, for 'The Poisoned Kiss' was that comic opera he dared not show to Holst, for that high-minded composer would never, Vaughan Williams tells us, have been able to understand how his friend could think it trivial and yet could want to write it. In this score Vaughan Williams displays a pretty musical ingenuity and wit of a delicacy one would hardly have expected him to possess.

The two choral works are 'Dona Nobis Pacem' and 'Five Tudor Portraits', works very different in subject and intention but alike in their broad confident sweep. The first is a passionate appeal for peace in which art and propaganda struggle for supremacy with somewhat confusing effect; the second is a riotous, ribald and romantic musical picture of five characters from poems by John Skelton. In both these works the power evident in the astonishing F minor Symphony remains, not in the form of surface violence, but disciplined and transmuted to make a solid foundation, apparent beneath even the most tranquil passages. This firm basis upon which the later music of Vaughan Williams rests recalls the architectural strength of Bach, the music itself the superb confidence of Handel.

'Dona Nobis Pacem' is a bewildering work. As a work of art it has everything against it. It is propaganda without a doubt; Vaughan Williams was here preoccupied with something momentarily more vital to him even than music, and he drives his message at us with the fervour of a nonconformist preacher. The text is as curious a patchwork as would be possible to devise, based upon a heterogeneous collection of biblical quotations — Jeremiah, Daniel and Haggai; Micah, Leviticus, the Psalms, Isaiah and Luke; embracing part of three poems by Walt Whitman, a passage from a political speech by John Bright (Vaughan Williams is nothing if not well-read), the whole concoction inserted between quotations in Latin from the Agnus Dei of the Mass. That a shortish cantata should be capable of digesting within itself so many different periods and styles of writing seems in the highest degree improbable, and the improbability is carried still further by the fact that, though the work was not completed until 1936, the longest section, Whitman's 'Dirge for Two Veterans', was composed long before the rest, as much earlier as before the Great War. It was a product of the Whitman - 'Sea' Symphony era and had been, for various reasons, consigned to a shelf for all those years. In spite of all this, 'Dona Nobis Pacem' does achieve, to my ears, a sort of unity. Vaughan Williams's message, melting and fusing in its passionate heat all the diverse elements that went to the music's construction, comes over with remarkable force, quite to the disregard of Messrs Bright, Haggai, Whitman, Jeremiah and the rest.

Faced with this unwieldy cantata, with its inconvenient appeal to emotions that music generally leaves in peace, I am at a loss to discover why it competes in my affections for a place alongside the works I cherish most, the 'Concerto Accademico', for instance, or 'Riders to the Sea'. I confess to a certain shame in making this admission. Critics have been tepid on the subject. Hubert Foss, in a book of some 200 pages long, allows it a bare half page of very faint praise. Nevertheless, where 'Dona Nobis Pacem' is to be performed there will I be also, if I can get there, to the probable neglect of some music of far greater purity and consistency. Quotations from the Mass and slices of the Bible suggest that this cantata is a religious one, but though the appeal of the soprano soloist is to Heaven the music never really ascends there. But what satisfying music it is, solid and rich! Here for once is a modern composer allowing us enough of every one of the beautiful themes. It is earthy music, its roots firmly planted in the soil; the music, one might say, if one did not already know it to be true, of a very large man. A reading of the text, which with the music is divided into six sections, certainly does not give the impression that this should be a happy work, and yet, curiously, that is the impression the music always leaves with me. Only the soprano soloist, and the women echoing her passionate appeal, show any sign of unsatisfaction. Their voices, sharp and anguished, contrast coldly with the positive richness and rhythm of the rest of the music. Using the same words, their cries recall the strained urgency of the lovely Agnus Dei of the Mass. The second, third and fourth episodes are Whitman's poems. The first, 'Beat, drums, beat!', bursts upon the soprano's pleading with a ruthless fury of percussion and brass. This section, delivered by the chorus, depicts the sweep of war upon the city. Its tragedy is swallowed up in exhilaration. 'Reconciliation', the second poem, is wholly calm and lovely:

> Word over all, beautiful as the sky,
> Beautiful that war and all its deeds of carnage must in time be utterly lost,
> That the hands of the sisters Death and Night incessantly,
> softly, wash again and ever again this soiled world.

Whitman's verse is enfolded in notes that follow, almost imperceptibly, the rhythm and cadence of the words, and which yet become a complete and rounded melody that could have been written by no other hand. The baritone soloist continues:

> For mine enemy is dead, a man divine as myself is dead,

and the chorus recapitulates the opening of the poem, like a benediction, expanding into eight-part harmony with a calm richness of texture unsurpassed in any choral music that I know.

'The Dirge for Two Veterans' which follows is probably, as has been objected, too long for the balance of the work. I would not relinquish one note of it. I settle myself deeper into my seat, shut my eyes, and hope it will go on for ever. The slow heavy march is established on the timpani. This, once set going, is dropped out

gradually, but the music pursues its steady course, leaving one's
inner ear to supply the beat. Into this unhurried measure Whitman's irregular lines are fitted with a variety of choral treatment;
women's voices alone sing the verse about the moon. After the
words — 'and the strong dead-march enwraps me' the chorus are
silent, letting the orchestra swell up into a complete statement of
the march tune. The chorus return to complete the poem. This
setting of the 'Dirge for Two Veterans' may be sung apart from
the rest of the cantata. Part five begins with John Bright's speech
and goes on to the Bible. Bright's words are delivered in recitative
over a rumble from the bass — 'The angel of Death has been
abroad throughout the land, you may almost hear the beating of
his wings.' The chorus break into anguished appeal. Their distress
is short-lived for the baritone is soon singing: 'O man, greatly
beloved, peace be unto thee; be strong.' The final episode, which
is Vaughan Williams's Biblical anthology, begins 'Nation shall not
lift up a sword against nation', and ends 'Glory to God in the
Highest, on Earth peace; goodwill towards men'. The whole
chorus and orchestra deliver this paean of praise, assisted finally by
the triumphal pealing of bells. Characteristically, though, Vaughan
Williams does not allow the work to end on this note of rapture.
When the praises have died away the soprano can be heard once
more reiterating, as if the whole cantata had never been, the words
of the opening and title — 'Dona Nobis Pacem'.

Everything that could not conveniently go into that cantata
found its way into 'Five Tudor Portraits', a remarkable bridging
of the years that separate John Skelton, Laureate, and tutor to
Henry VIII, from our own day. The Tudor priest of scandalous
and apocryphal private life had almost as many facets to his poetic
art as Vaughan Williams has to his music. Racy, ribald and rum-
bustious in one poem, tenderly romantic in another; at times
scorching the church of the period with his satire; at others
prostrate in reverent adoration before his crucified God; Skelton
is Vaughan Williams's natural collaborator. Skelton, to readers of
today, can seem astonishingly modern; Vaughan Williams is quite
sufficiently Tudor for there to be no need for either to shift his

ground to accommodate the other. They meet on the common ground of their English heritage, neither bearing any resemblance to the traditional portrait of the Englishman, and sharing a strain of rich romance which is far too shameless ever to become senti-mental. The composer, in this work, has represented all the facets of the remarkable character of this Rector of Diss, except the religious. The Skelton of such poems as 'Wofully Araid' is not here. He would be out of place in such an extrovert work. Yet how wonderfully Vaughan Williams might interpret him.

Though this choral suite comes obviously from the mind that found music for Falstaff there are no folk-songs in this score, hardly even the echoes of them. It is true that the famous flattened sevenths are well in evidence. 'Sie haben eine Leidenschaft für die kleine Septime,' Max Bruch had complained. I suppose I must have a Leidenschaft for it too, because it is always after Vaughan Williams has perpetrated some that I discover all over again how much he is my favourite composer. The begetter of the F minor Symphony, though, is as much in evidence as the hand that wrote 'Sir John — '. I cannot avoid a feeling of impatience with a com-poser who can turn out music of such superlative confidence, of such subtlety and wit as are to be found in this score, and then con-tinue to accuse himself of lack of technique and amateurishness. The hand of the amateur is, perhaps, noticeable in the stitching together of the diverse elements in 'Dona Nobis Pacem', but 'Five Tudor Portraits' is as professional a work as the almost forbid-dingly professional 'Job'.

'I have ventured to take some liberties with the text,' Vaughan Williams writes in his usual prefatory note. 'In doing this I am aware that I have laid myself open to the accusation of cutting out somebody's "favourite bit". If any omissions are to be made this, I fear, is inevitable. On the whole I have managed to keep in all my own "favourite bits" though there are certain passages which I have omitted unwillingly. The omissions are due partly to the great length of the original, partly because some passages did not lend themselves to musical treatment and partly because certain lines which would sound well when spoken cannot conveniently

be sung.' There is a fourth reason which Dr Vaughan Williams
does not mention. Skelton's pen was too ribald and outspoken for
our weak modern stomachs. No singer would sing him unexpur-
gated. Indeed even some of the lines in 'Elinor Rumming' which
the composer has allowed to stand sound oddly enough sung by a
choir of white- or black-clad ladies and gentlemen in boiled shirts.

Each movement has its formal musical title as well as the title of
Skelton's poem above it. 'The Tunning of Elinor Rumming,'
described as a Ballad, introduces us to the hostess of an unsavoury
tavern in Leatherhead, a town around which Vaughan Williams
had collected some beautiful folk-songs; and also to the rabble
who resorted there to drink her 'nappy ale'. The movement is a
headlong chase through a breathless multitude of rhythms and a
scheme of tonality calculated to keep the most learned musico-
logist guessing. Skelton's lines are of a monotonous cut:

> Tell you I will
> If that ye will
> Awhile be still
> Of a comely Jill
> That dwelt on a hill.

is a fair sample. This fact, that would strike terror to the heart of
a poetry reader, stimulated Vaughan Williams to the devising of a
variety of unexpected rhythmic patterns which sound, nevertheless, perfectly natural. The chorus introduces the lady, after a crashing opening motto theme, to a three-four march, 'allegro pesante'
(surely Vaughan Williams's favourite rhythm):

> Droopy and drowsy,
> Scurvy and lowsy,
> Her face all bowsy,
> Comely crinkled,
> Wondrously wrinkled,
> Like a roast pig's ear
> Bristled with hair.

The women in Vaughan Williams's operas are almost all enchanting, and the three whose portraits he draws in this suite are no

exception to that rule. In his hands even Elinor is delightful. 'Her viságe', declared Skelton, 'would assuage a man's couráge.' Vaughan Williams is made of sterner stuff, for, after the first precipitate exposition, ending with a few energetic bars of march-tune for the orchestra alone, he hesitates, pauses a moment, and, with a modulation and the incongruous word 'grazioso' written over the music, he melts into a waltz tune, as pretty a waltz tune as any composer of popular music could invent. Thus, charmingly, the chorus detail Elinor's apparel. Nevertheless, the conclusion reached at the end of this delightful interlude, which is interspersed throughout with flourishes that recall the more recherché percussion in Walton's 'Belshazzar's Feast', is that 'the devil and she be sib'.

The tempo changes to allegro and the time signature to nine-eight as the interest is transferred from the hostess to her clients:

> *Cisly and Sare*
> *With their legs bare.*
> *They run in haste*
> *Unbraced and unlaced,*
> *Their kirtles all jagged,*
> *Their smoks all to-ragged,*
> *With titters and tatters*
> *Bring dishes and platters,*
> *With all their might running*
> *To Elinor Rumming*
> *To have of her tunning.*

We are dragged willy-nilly, 'thorough bush, thorough briar', through a multiplicity of key signatures — from B minor, through D minor, to G minor. Then suddenly into the major, past C and A and F, to E flat, back to C, and ending up in B flat. Breathless, we are left to recover ourselves, while the bassoon, 'senza misura', 'doloroso' and, mercifully, 'andante' introduces yet another lady — Drunken Alice. This is a solo for the contralto, and her gossip, before she is overcome with the ale and falls asleep, is of the strangest:

> *Of tidings in Wales,*
> *And of St James in Gales,*
> *And of the Portingales.*

She suffers from hiccups and from catarrh:

> *Snivelling in her nose*
> *As if she had the pose.*

and the orchestra assist her along with a doleful jazz. When she drops off, to a snore from the double bassoon, the chorus resort to another headlong measure, beginning faint and far, but gaining strength and ending up carolling 'Tirley tirlow' for all they are worth. Author and composer suddenly decide:

> *But my fingers itch*
> *I have written too much.*

and, with another reference to Elinor's angular 'motto', bring the movement to an abrupt end. This 'mad mumming' sometimes recalls a chorus out of 'Hugh the Drover', but in the 'Tudor Portraits' there is nothing false or dutiful about the boisterousness. The composer's enjoyment is as robust as the poet's and he knows full well how to put it into his music.

Full well, also, by this date, does he know how to twist the heartstrings by the simplest modulation, the most apparently straightforward of harp glissandos, or merely by the juxtaposition of two such differing atmospheres as the rampageous interior of the inn at Leatherhead and the summer beauty of the Intermezzo that follows. 'Pretty Bess' is one of Vaughan Williams's ingénues — a sister for Anne Page or for Tormentilla of 'The Poisoned Kiss':

> *My daisy delectable,*
> *My primrose commendable,*
> *My violet amiable,*
> *My joy inexplicable.*

and he weaves around her music as delicious as either of those heroines enjoys. Introduced by the oboe, the baritone sings the five-verse poem, while the chorus echo the refrain, sometimes in step with him, sometimes lagging behind, but catching up at the last verse to finish neatly with him. The oboe appropriates the singer's phrase 'My proper Bess, my pretty Bess' and uses it to decorate the stanzas with its own variations. But Bess is not entirely kind and the baritone declares himself 'disdained, and as a man half maimed', his heart is 'so sore pained', and the lovely melody is only half happy. This music, simultaneously sad and happy, is the old simple love music of the operas, deriving its heart-rending sweetness from Vaughan Williams's determination to enjoy, in one tune, the best of both worlds at once — the major and the minor.

There is no lamentation whatever during the following Burlesca — 'An Epitaph on John Jayberd of Diss' — which is as far as can be from the mourning that its title suggests. It is a hearty, noisy and unfeeling rejoicing, by the men of the chorus, at the demise of a most deplorable cleric — John Jayberd, 'a man renowned for malice, double hearted and double tongued, worn out with old age, suspected of all, loved by none'. The chorus race through this trental, mostly in a curious rhymed Latin, but with an odd line of English thrown in here and there, at the speed of an express train, applying the brakes suddenly and raspingly once or twice to deliver, with horrid emphasis, their more insulting comments. 'Jam jacet hic' they declare, with a startling vocal glissando, 'stark dead, Never a tooth in his head,' and they fall to a cheerful drinking song:

> With fill, fill, fill, the black bowl
> For Jayberd's soul . . .
> With hey ho, rumbelow,
> Rumpopulorum.

and end 'maestoso' with a sudden parody of the Holy Office, 'Per omnia secula seculorum', while the orchestra gives its own final Presto comment.

The sombre 'cello, 'lento doloroso', is the first to lift its voice in support of 'Jane Scroop — her Lament for Philip Sparrow', contributing its tone to a twenty-minute movement in which each separate instrument waits on the composer's summons to add its exact nuance of interpretation to Skelton's lines. Jane Scroop was a schoolgirl, educated in the convent of the 'Black Nuns' at Carrow, whose playmate sparrow had been cruelly slain by 'Gib, our cat'. Vaughan Williams chooses to align himself beside the child in her sorrow — 'Jane saw no reason and I see no reason why she should not pray for the peace of her sparrow's soul,' he writes, brushing aside any suggestion that the poem might be taken as a burlesque; but he preserves throughout an exquisite balance between heartfelt grief and the most delicate of fantasy. His tongue is not for one moment in his cheek, but his wit and invention are on the stretch to catch the smallest subtlety of this sweet and solemn verse and turn it to musical account. For all its sincere solemnity the title Romanza is exact.

Eschewing the obvious choice of a soprano for the schoolgirl Jane, he made a contralto his soloist and wrote for the altos of his chorus music so pleasurable in its subdued and rounded contours as to compensate them for many years of playing second fiddle to the sopranos. In this way he has pitched the whole movement into a shadowed mellowness of tone which affords a perfect background for the birds that, later, are to twitter and sing against its velvet texture. Women's voices only are used, the chorus representing, one assumes, the Nuns of Carrow, but sounding very young, for all the dominance of alto tone, as if it were a bunch of novices who join with Jane in her sparrow's solemn requiem. The poem begins in lamentation and with the calling down of vengeance:

> On the whole nation
> Of cattes wild and tame.
> (God send them sorrow and shame!)

But Jane was very young, and her reminiscences, as children's will, lead her from time to time away from sorrow, and, the composer following with exquisite instrumental illustration, she dwells happily on the remembrance of Philip's little habits:

> Sometime he would gasp
> When he saw a wasp.

A fly or a gnat
He would fly at that.
And prettily he would pant
When he saw an ant.
Lord, how he would pry
After the butterfly!
Lord, how he would hop
After the grasshop!

and the ant, the butterfly, the grasshop, run, fly and skip through
the orchestra. But happiness is fleeting and once more the chorus
and Jane raise their voices in a great wail:

Alas, it wil me slo
That Philip is gone me fro!

the 'cello returning to their support to finish this section of the
movement as he began it.

Now muted trumpets and woodwinds give out a fanfare and
Jane, depersonalised, takes her part as celebrant at Philip's requiem:

Lauda, anima mea, Dominum,
To weep with me look that ye come,
All manner of birdes in your kind,
See none be left behind.

Her voice is like a trumpet call. And how they come — chirping,
twittering, warbling — the flute; the oboe; the clarinet; the brass,
muted — in a symphony of bird noises that resembles nothing
that Vaughan Williams had ever written before! When they are
assembled the chorus assign to them their respective roles:

Robin Redbreast he shall be the priest
The requiem mass to sing . . .
The duck and the drake
Shall watch at his wake;
The owl that is so foul
Will help us to howl.

This works up to a mysterious passage over an accompaniment
that resembles the horrific opening bars of the F minor Symphony,

at the climax of which the contralto is suddenly left alone singing fortissimo:

> *Libera me domine*
> *In doh la sol re —*

the most astonishing piece of Puccini Vaughan Williams ever perpetrated — a sequence ready-made that might have come straight out of 'Turandot', used by the composer with obvious relish. After this staggering passage the movement sinks back into its former shadowed beauty with a slow hymn, 'tranquillo', sung in four-part harmony, while the hollow voice of the horn mourns underneath:

> *And now the dark cloudy night*
> *Chaseth away Phoebus bright*
> *Taking his course towards the west*
> *God send my sparrow's soul good rest,*

while Jane, half singing, half speaking, continues her plainsong chant. As this serene twilight elegy is lulling us to sleep it changes suddenly to a perky little tune, Philip's own tune:

> *For he was a pretty cock*
> *And came of a gentle stock,*

recalling to us suddenly the small object of all this heavy mourning, almost forgotten in the midst of such high solemnity. It is unbearably, enchantingly pathetic, and hits one right below the belt. According to the score the 'cello now returns to join with the voices as they sink down into a peaceful darkness, but I have been rendered temporarily numb with sorrow and have no recollection of ever actually hearing the last page of this most lovely movement, after the heart-rending repetition of the sparrow's own little theme.

'Jolly Rutterkin', the Scherzo, is a sudden plunge into cold water — salutary, refreshing, but not, until the breath comes back, entirely pleasant. 'Rutterkin', whom I knew in Skelton's poem a decade before I discovered Vaughan Williams's music, was never one of my favourite characters; nor do I fall for the composer's attempt to make us identify the rogue of unseemly habits:

In a cloak without a gown
Save a ragged hood to cover his crown,

with the gentleman from the song out of 'Magnificence' who was:

Properly dressed
All point devise

And who could say of himself:

Beyond measure
My sleeve is wide,
All of pleasure
My hose straight tied,
My buskin wide
Rich to behold
Glittering in gold.

Not that it matters!

'Five Tudor Portraits' began with a movement that visited every key under the sun, dragging in accidental sharps and flats regardless. It ends with a movement into which only a solitary accidental strays, and that with small effect. The plain downrightness of the major key contributes to its strength, its sweep, its brilliance and also, to my mind, its inflexibility. It is bright with fanfares. It does not spare the ear. The baritone, singing his swaggering verse, has almost as great a contrast with his lover of 'Pretty Bess' as the contralto has between Drunken Alice and Jane Scroop. After the twenty minutes given to Philip Sparrow, Rutterkin is allowed less than five. But it is enough of this hard and virile music, a sufficient, suitable conclusion to a major work, a stimulating epilogue to speed the departing concert-goer happily on his homeward way.

In this suite the several streams of Vaughan Williams's musical styles run together — the solidity and vigour of 'Job'; the 'take it or leave it' modernity of the last symphony; the unexpected witty subtlety of the songs in 'The Poisoned Kiss'; and with these there is a new freedom and relaxation, a shameless lyrical enjoyment and, at last, a full measure of that robust and impolite humour that had been lurking under the surface of several earlier works, but never till now — not even in 'Sir John — ' had been allowed a completely free rein.

1937 was the year of the Coronation of King George VI. Much of the music of our Coronation Service is there by tradition, much of it is new; but the Te Deum, which is the musical and emotional climax of the ceremony, is always the commissioned work of a living composer. That year the choice fell on Vaughan Williams. The ceremony of Coronation is long and tiring; exhausting to the participants; nerve-racking to the musicians; a considerable ordeal for the audience who have been inside the Abbey since dawn. It is even tiring for those who can only sit at home and listen to their wireless. After the climax of the crowning and the homage, when the anointed sovereign retires into a side chapel to exchange St Edward's heavy crown for the splendour of the Imperial State Crown, both nerves and ears alike demand a release of a fanfare of bright sound. Music is demanded to rouse the echoes and make the very stones cry out for joy; the kind of music Dryden and Milton described so often and so feelingly; 'the saintly shout and solemn jubily' imputed to the saints in Heaven. This Vaughan Williams understood very well. I only wish that the heraldic splendour and simplicity of this Te Deum (from 'traditional material') could now be admitted to the service for ever alongside Handel's 'Zadok the Priest' and Parry's 'I was glad — '. In 1953, when the turn of Sir William Walton came, the Te Deum failed in its effect because it was over-complicated. Fine music as it has since proved itself to be in other services and in the concert hall, the exhausted ear and mind simply could not take it in and the long-awaited climax of pure joy was never achieved. Vaughan Williams set his Te Deum for choir, organ and trumpets. The clear bright string of 'praise Hims', divided from each other by crashing fanfares, remains for ever in one's memory of that service. The middle section, 'when Thou tookest upon Thee to deliver man — ,' tender though it is, hardly slackens the forward impulse of the strongly rhythmic music towards the last terrific fanfare, after which the choir, un-accompanied, sing 'Let me never be confounded' to a dying phrase of exquisite shapelessness.

Fanfares, too, of a very different nature, come threading their way up through the lovely moonlit texture of the 'Serenade to Music' — 'the horns of Elfland faintly blowing,' though the text here is not Tennyson but Shakespeare. This music was written for another festival occasion — the seventieth birthday of Sir Henry Wood, and it has no parallel in all Vaughan Williams's work, or, indeed, in anybody else's, though it stems from the new style of sweet enchantment he invented for Jane Scroop and her sparrow. Sir Henry set the composer a pretty problem, for he asked for music containing parts for sixteen famous singers whose careers had frequently been associated with his own throughout his long life as a conductor. Vaughan Williams tackled the problem in what was both the most obvious and the most difficult way. Dispensing altogether with chorus, he composed a work for sixteen soloists and orchestra in which the soloists themselves supplied the chordal passages. Moreover, with a charming delicacy of touch, he wrote for each singer music particularly calculated to bring out the individual quality of their voice. In the absence of any of those original sixteen soloists the full perfection of the Serenade can never be recaptured. What we hear now can only be a second best. Perhaps as the Serenade was the most personal and loving of birthday gifts we should be content that this should be so.

If beauty is to be reckoned in terms of what is shapely, sweet, flowing, harmonious, then the 'Serenade to Music' is the most beautiful music Vaughan Williams ever wrote. The individual colours of the orchestral instruments are weighed against each other with the same precision as each individual singer's voice is allotted the one or two solo phrases that are the most so short a work can allow. Each separate voice, each instrument, pays its tribute to the conductor and then blends into deliciously calculated harmony.

> *How sweet the moonlight sleeps upon this bank!*
> *Here will we sit and let the sounds of music*
> *Creep in our ears —*

Lorenzo's words to Jessica. And how sweetly they creep! 'The touches of sweet harmony' enriching the long melody that is the Serenade's main theme; the fanfares magically interrupting before the beauty of that theme has time to surfeit us.

The text, selected rather piecemeal from the Belmont scene of *The Merchant of Venice*, is a paean to music in silence and the night — 'methinks it sounds much sweeter than by day' — and this Serenade is night music if ever music was. The composer who has confessed 'I usually feel content to provide good plain cooking' has been more than usually liberal with the sweetening of this particular dish. We have now become familiar with the unusual number of different styles which are each one the natural medium of his musical expression, sometimes several of them, each distinct, set alongside in one work, as in the 'Tudor Portraits' and in 'Job'. It would be a fascinating occupation to classify everything he has ever written under one or other of five or six separate headings — the secular operatic tunefulness; the rich nobility of the religious music; the downright discordant modernism of Satan and the F minor Symphony. The 'Serenade to Music' stands quite alone. In the loveliness of its melody and the limpidity of its harmony there is not a trace of religious exaltation, yet it is quite different from his operatic flights of Puccini-like ecstasy. It even has a sadness, recalling Bax or Delius, the clue to which, perhaps, is given in Jessica's words: 'I am never merry when I hear sweet music', words which set the mood of the whole Serenade, but which one can hardly imagine Vaughan Williams would ever say himself. Humour creeps in at the first opportunity when, with successively deeper voices, following the one upon the other, the men tell in horrified tones of 'the man who has no music in himself' over a grinding, disapproving bass.

The 'Serenade to Music' illustrates a curious truth; that beauty pure and simple is not really what we want from music, in spite of our continual cries against the ugliness of what is modern. This work is universally admired and loved among musicians. I have never met one who was not almost reverent in his praise of it. But the ordinary listener who happens to enjoy Vaughan Williams's music does not get on with it so well. This is a very strange thing, for the Serenade is as easy on the ear as music can be — designedly so, I imagine, for a festival piece ought to be capable of instant enjoyment. For myself, I find it over-sweet and it is only in a rare mood that I can 'take' it. Then, I must admit, it is as ravishing as any concord of sweet sounds can be. It is music written 'con amore', as deeply felt and carefully considered as the music of any of the symphonies.

'Con amore' could be written also over the score of the 'Five Variants of Dives and Lazarus' for string orchestra and harp. At the New York World Fair of 1939 the music of all nations was represented in new compositions by their most eminent composers. While most of those chosen to represent the musical life of England sat down and composed large-scale symphonies and concertos, the oldest and the greatest of them, in a manner typically infuriating, quietly went back to his first love the folk-song and produced this mellow and haunting meditation on the various versions of one of the most beautiful of them. One version of this tune, from Miss Lucy Broadwood's collection, had been stored in Vaughan Williams's mind for many years, for in 1906 he arranged it for *The English Hymnal* to replace the lachrymose horror which had formerly been the tune of 'I heard the voice of Jesus say — '. A variant, as he explains in a note attached to the score, is the name given by musicians to the different versions of the same tune that turn up mysteriously not only in different parts of the same country, but sometimes from places far across the seas. The note states that none of these five variants exactly corresponds to any one known version of the tune. The first full-bodied statement of this melody is the one that most of us find we have known all our lives, whether we discovered it in *The English Hymnal*, or *Songs of Praise*, or, set to very different words, in the *Oxford Book of Carols* (all three books part-edited by Vaughan Williams), or have simply known it in our bones from birth or earlier. 'Dives and Lazarus' is a rounded, mellow, near-sentimental tune with a touch of pleasant melancholy — not in the least the early-morning-dew type of folk-song, and it cries out for the full richness of 'cello and viola tone, the deep murmur of the basses, the golden stream of decoration that only the harp could supply. Vaughan Williams has set it in a glory of autumnal colour.

Here in 1939 on the threshold of another war, and with the ancient tune of 'Dives and Lazarus' echoing in our memory, it might be worth while to pause for a moment in our journey and look back over the past years; not at the long procession of symphonies, operas and cantatas that we have been considering up till now, but at the innumerable small things that Vaughan Williams found time to fit in among his larger works, and, in particular, at those three books of which he was the musical editor. His preface to the first of these, *The English Hymnal*, though written before he had composed many of the works we now remember, reveals his commonsense and downright attitude to the art of music as a whole, an attitude he has maintained all his life in public utterance and private teaching. It is a great pity that the Church has not seen fit to adopt his suggestions wholesale, for our services would by now be very different. As early as this preface, 1906, for instance, he declared war against those appalling marks of expression that still disfigure every verse of *Hymns A & M*, requiring one, with disastrous effect, to sing perhaps three words 'pianissimo' in the middle of a 'forte' line. 'Another painful experience', he writes, 'is to hear an organist trying to play through a C.M. or L.M. tune in absolutely strict time, regardless of the slight pause which the congregation with unconscious artistic insight are inclined to make at the end of every line.' In these hymn-books, relying a good deal more on this 'unconscious artistic insight' with which he credits us than on the good sense that clergymen or organists ought to be supposed to possess, he labours to clear away some of the 'miasma of languishing and sentimental tunes, which so often disfigure our service'. 'The usual argument in favour of bad music', he writes, 'is that the fine tunes are doubtless "musically correct" but that the people want "something simple". Now the expression "musically correct" has no meaning; the only "correct" music is that which is beautiful and noble.'

Two of his own 'beautiful and noble' hymns — two only so far among a dozen or more in the hymn-books — have established themselves in the regular repertoire of every congregation and are as natural to them as the 'Old Hundredth' or 'Onward, Christian Soldiers'. Nobody is now unhappy singing 'For all the saints — ' or 'Come Down, O Love Divine,' so long as they do not discover that the composer is alive. I have known a person to be made very unhappy indeed by the discovery that the latter tune — 'Down Ampney' — was by a living composer of his own nationality and not, as he had supposed, by a contemporary of Palestrina. It had been his favourite hymn. I doubt if he ever enjoyed it again. There are a number of excellent tunes besides Vaughan Williams's few in these hymn-books still waiting for an enterprising organist to introduce them to the congregation. It is only necessary to slip a new tune into the service on alternate Sundays for a couple of months to persuade the congregation that they have always known it, however hard they may resist on the first two occasions. It is infuriating to find a church (I have known examples) that goes to the trouble and expense of buying countless copies of a new hymn-book and then retains in the organ loft a copy of *A & M* out of which the old discarded tune is played, because nobody has the guts to face the inevitable grumbles of the older members of the congregation when they are introduced to anything slightly unfamiliar. Have the younger members no rights? Many of them were introduced to better tunes at school, and if they are driven out of the churches by the poverty of the music it is not the fault of those who compiled the hymn-books. Good hymn tunes have been at the disposal of the Church since 1906. The small use to which they have been put stirs me to such bad temper that it would be wiser, I think, to move quickly on to pleasanter matters.

Vaughan Williams's contributions to the *Oxford Book of Carols* are very pleasant matters. This collection was published in 1928 and contains many arrangements under the initials R.V.W. There are four original songs; two of them cradle songs, one to words by Blake, one to words by Wither, both gentle, tenderly austere; 'The Golden Carol', an antique unison frolic, and 'Snow in the Street' to a poem by William Morris which exercises a compelling hypnotism in a tune that, turning round and round upon itself, is infinitely unwilling ever to stop.

At first Vaughan Williams had been doubtful whether he might be wasting his time in sacrificing to the 1906 *Hymnal* two years that might have been devoted to 'original' work. 'But I know now', he writes, 'that two years of close contact with some of the best (as well as some of the worst) tunes in the world was a better musical education than any amount of sonatas and fugues.'

There were settings, too, of folk-songs arranged for unaccompanied chorus, providing, as I can testify from experience, every voice with music that is good to sing. Among his own original songs the listener may well be growing tired of 'Linden Lea', which had paid the price of its own excellence, but there are many others, and nobody can deny the wistful beauty of those long phrases. There are motets. I have rarely known such pure pleasure as I found in taking part in the wonderful 'Valiant-for-Truth' with its free-rhythmed plainsong line moving unhurriedly towards the terrific passage — 'And all the trumpets sounded for him on the other side', when the entire chorus turn into human trumpets for the most triumphant passage, perhaps, that he ever composed. This is a big work and perhaps the most perfect that his long connection with 'The Pilgrim's Progress' produced.

Mention should be made somewhere — and why not here? — of the purely orchestral works based on folk-songs written at intervals throughout Vaughan Williams's life, works such as the 'Folk-Song Suite' that are as familiar to listeners who do not know the name Vaughan Williams as his overture to 'The Wasps' has now become, and without which producers of plays and features in the B.B.C. could hardly do their work. The 'Folk-Song Suite' itself, with its stimulating march movements 'Seventeen Come Sunday' and 'Folk-Songs from Somerset', and between them the sad enchanting 'My Bonny Boy' with its echo of Butterworth, was, in fact, written for military band. The orchestral version we know so well is actually the work of Dr Gordon Jacob, of whom Vaughan Williams wrote — 'He was at one time nominally my pupil, though there was nothing I could teach him which he did

not know better than I, at all events in the matter of technique.'
His adaptation of this most typically Vaughan Williams work is
so perfectly in tune with its creator that his part in the music is
rarely given any acknowledgement.

The 'Running Set', an interwoven collection of folk-dances put
together for a dance found in North America which had lost its
tune, seems to have called forth little comment from the critics.
When played with determination by a very large orchestra it
reaches such a pitch of rhythmic excitement that it seems to me to
do for the folk-dance what Ravel's music did for 'La Valse', creating a state of emotional tension that is (a rare condition in Vaughan
Williams's music) almost purely physical. It makes the feet itch to
dance. I have never before suspected folk-dancing of being capable of such desperate abandon, and, since hearing it, have looked
upon folk-dancers with a good deal more interest.

The only Norfolk Rhapsody that remains to us contains three
songs: 'A Bold Young Sailor', 'On Board the 98' and 'The Captain's Apprentice'. Though in the middle it bursts into a cheerful
rhythm like the marches in the 'Folk-Song Suite', it begins and
ends with the sort of dreamy impressionistic music that was extended into the Symphonic Impression — 'In the Fen Country'
— and which, in the end, became the basis of the 'Pastoral' Symphony. Vividly it recreates the flat land of East Anglia, which
district would seem to have had a more lasting effect on the
pictorial landscape painting of Vaughan Williams's music than the
lusher beauty of his own Gloucestershire. In connection with 'The
Norfolk Rhapsody' this is, perhaps, the moment to deplore that
artistic integrity that compels him to 'scrap' any of his early writings that do not quite come up to his present exacting standard.

The second war to interrupt Vaughan Williams's long life of
composing did not make quite the demands of the first. He was
sixty-seven at its outbreak and producing music with increasing
fluency. This he continued to do to our comfort and solace, and
there is no gap in the list of his works such as was occasioned by
the earlier war. Yet he undertook a variety of war-time duties:
the collection of salvage, an occupation only a degree less menial

than his floor-scrubbing activities of the earlier war; and the chair-
manship of a Home Office Board to supervise the release of in-
terned foreign musicians. His writings reveal him as irritated that
he was not allowed to take a more active part. He turned his hand
to the composition of music for films. He has described, in an
essay, 'Composing for Films', now published in his book of collected papers, *Some Thoughts on Beethoven's Choral Symphony with
writings on other musical subjects*, how he came to 'have a shot' at
this exacting art. It was by his own wish, not surprisingly, for he
would be the last person to leave any avenue of musical expression
unexplored. But he owns himself shaken when, as a result of expressing that wish, a film conductor telephoned him on a Saturday
requiring a film score by the following Wednesday. It is surprising that he should have made such an outstanding success of his
film music, not through any lack of technique, whatever he would
have us believe, but because one would have imagined the discipline to have been irksome to such an individual artist. His way,
evidenced in the texts of 'Dona Nobis Pacem' and 'Sir John in
Love', has always been to batter his material forcibly into the shape
he desired, but in films the opposite procedure is forced upon the
composer. The music must be tailored to fit the lengths of film.
He writes, however, 'Film composing is a splendid discipline,'
and could say in 1945, 'Some of my more practised colleagues
assure me that when I have had all their experience my youthful
exuberance will disappear, and I shall look upon film composing
not as an art but as a business. At present I still feel a morning
blush which has not yet paled into the light of common day. I
still believe the film contains potentialities for the combination of
all the arts such as Wagner never dreamt of.'

His scores were masterly, in one or two cases lifting a mediocre
script into distinction, only occasionally overpowering the film
altogether. Finally in 1948 the score commissioned by Ealing
Studios for *Scott of the Antarctic* started something in his mind that
would not let him rest until, in 1952, it emerged as the colossal
'Sinfonia Antartica'. I listened to these film scores, I have to
admit, with my eyes occasionally shut in case the film for which

they were supposed merely to be the background might detract from my enjoyment of the music. I was deeply suspicious of my favourite composer's new-found enthusiasm, fearing for all the music that might be lost for ever. I need not have worried. Vaughan Williams is no more willing than his hearers to lose sight of a good idea. Apart from the 'Scott' music, he has himself come to the rescue of the majestic prelude to his first feature film — 49th Parallel — and set it to a song 'The New Commonwealth'. Another theme from the film is translated most gratefully to be the theme of the Scherzo of his mellifluous A minor Quartet.

In 1944, before that string quartet, Vaughan Williams published another quartet and gave it the title 'Household Music'. This meditation, in the form of three preludes on the Welsh hymn tunes 'Crug-y-bar', 'St Denio', and 'Aberystwyth', is scored for string quartet, but 'the composer has envisaged their being played by almost any combination of instruments which may be gathered together at one time in a household'. I have heard this music only on the strings for which it was 'principally designed', and I would give much to be present at some performance in which some of the 'flutes, recorders, oboes, bassoons, euphonium'; 'clarinets, cornet, saxophone or saxhorns', not to mention the 'ad lib' horn, for which a special part has been written, could be heard in any combination whatsoever.

My first hearing of this music was unexpected and, because of the incongruity of the setting, immensely moving. An earnest and extremely competent quartet of three Frenchmen and an Armenian played it in a small French town to celebrate, in a concert of music by the allies, the anniversary of the end of the war. Since I was the only English person present I received the enthusiastic congratulations of the players on possessing a composer who could write a work so delightful to play and a musical tradition that could throw up three such splendid tunes.

Welsh hymn tunes were never my favourites; they lack the feel of out-of-doors and make me think of harmoniums and the smell of oil lamps; but the loving handling to which they are subjected in this quartet has made me an unwilling convert to, at any rate, these three. 'Crug-y-bar', subtitled here 'Fantasia', is number 609 in *Songs of Praise*, set to the hymn 'O Sing to the Lord now, His Greatness — '. The notes appended to the hymn-book describe its syncopated rhythm and its pentatonic melody as adding up to qualities of 'rude vigour' and 'primitive grandeur'. Better known is the theme of the Scherzo, 'St Denio', 'Immortal, invisible God, only wise — ' based on a Welsh folk-song; and even better still 'Aberystwyth', the theme of the last movement, a set of eight variations. Belonging in all hymn-books, the old as well as the new, to the words 'Jesu, Lover of my soul — ' it is indeed so well known that *Songs of Praise Discussed*, while spending two thickly-printed pages upon the words, says of the tune only that it 'needs no comment'. Liking this tune the least of the three — probably because it is so heartily approved by those who blindly cling to *A & M* — I find myself enjoying this the most of the three preludes. It has a persuasive rolling flow, initiated by that characteristic five-quaver upward phrase that recurs three times in the original tune and seems to dominate the eight variations.

To look at the score is to long to take part in it, even on a comb and tissue paper. Splendid and conducive to national pride though it was in the setting of a sort of miniature Covent Garden where I first heard it, I feel that it must sound at its best in the surroundings for which it was designed; played, no matter how stumblingly, and phrases gone over again and again, not only for practice but to extract the last drop of their beauty, with, perhaps, the crackling of a log fire to replace the horn part, in some ambitiously musical household. How much more pleasure might we all derive from an evening spent disentangling and putting together the strands of this simple but intricately counterpointed music, than from going out to hear other people making expert music for our entertainment in concert halls. The 'Household Music' is homespun and well-christened. Vaughan Williams is fond of the analogy of the ' "humus" which alone can fertilise the great flower that blooms but once in a hundred years'. It is out of the rich compost of such small works that his own great symphonies rise.

And, appropriately, one such was to bloom in the summer of

the next year. The Symphony in D, his fifth, was performed during the Promenade season of 1943. It met with an immediate acceptance from public and musicians alike, extremely rare for a modern work, and was elevated — or reduced — at once to the level of a popular classic, going the mysterious way that fifth symphonies seem to go, along with those of Beethoven, Tchaikovsky, Dvořák, Sibelius and even, at a later date, Rubbra! It became surrounded with a miasma of non-musical emotions and associations which threatened to obscure or completely stifle the music itself. The symphony's way had been prepared by the celebrations in October 1942 of the composer's seventieth birthday. The B.B.C. in a series nominally of six concerts, but actually of many more, extended over a period of several months, must have introduced Vaughan Williams to a vast public previously almost unconscious of his existence, and in a mood particularly ready to accept him. Orchestras large and small all over the country seized the occasion to do honour to him by including his works in their programmes. For a time his music was really difficult to escape. Among a series of talks on the composer the B.B.C. let slip the information that a new symphony was on the way. We had rather more than six months to wait for it and too much anticipation is very unsettling. The longer one looks forward to music the less sanely is one able to listen to it in the end. The occasion of its first performance was only too ripe. The war seemed to have been going on for an interminable length of time. For us at home the stage it had reached was infinitely boring. There were not even any air-raids to keep us on our toes. We were thoroughly fed-up. So we stood in the Prom or sat back in as much comfort as is possible in the Albert Hall, and, paying little attention to the means employed to make this divine noise, soaked up its message of heavenly consolation.

In case, as at the time we liked to imagine, anybody still thinks this music was offered us as a form of escape from grim reality, it is as well to remember that it was begun before the war and that certain of its themes had their origin in the opera 'The Pilgrim's Progress' on which Vaughan Williams had been at work intermittently for many years and which, it was rumoured, he had abandoned. Once more Vaughan Williams was heralded as a prophet, whose Symphony in F minor of 1935 forecast the horrors of war and whose new Symphony in D with all its radiance and comfort could be taken as a picture of post-war bliss. Both history and the composer, with his later E minor Symphony, gave us something of a slap in the face, exposing this view of the matter as sentimental and inaccurate in the extreme.

There was another suggestion fostered by some of the most reputable critics who wrote about this work, which was depressing at the time, particularly to one like myself who had only recently woken up to the knowledge that a mighty genius was in our midst; and which now appears delightfully funny. These critics implied that this symphony was an inevitable return to an earlier mood and style, that it was a summing-up of everything that had gone before and was almost a farewell. Vaughan Williams, in the proper course of time, went on to celebrate his eightieth birthday, with a sixth symphony behind him and a seventh up his sleeve, neither of them remotely akin to the D major in style. A glance at the size and variety of the compositions that fill these ten years makes these notices very amusing reading indeed.

Having, in the emotion of the moment, heard this symphony all wrong to start with, having loved it and wearied of it through injudicious indulgence; thought it the greatest thing Vaughan Williams had ever given us and then wondered if it was not perhaps the least interesting of the symphonies, I made a great effort to get to know it all over again. With a score and gramophone records and a mind as empty of past associations as I could make it I set out to woo it once more. The enterprise was triumphantly successful and proved to me for ever the absolute falsity of the amateur view that the more you know about the way music is produced the less beauty and magic you find in it. The cold black print of the score revealed miracles to my ear that it had only half appreciated in the concert hall. I realised to my shame that I had never really heard this symphony.

The dedication over the score originally read 'without permission and in sincerest flattery, to Jean Sibelius, whose great example is worthy of every imitation'. This was enough to send everybody to that Prom with their ears pricked to detect echoes of the great Finnish composer in Vaughan Williams's work: but there is only one passage, a great windy rushing of strings in the development of the first movement, that could conceivably bear his influence. The music is typical Vaughan Williams throughout, compounded, if one wishes to make such an analysis, of elements from 'Job', the 'Pastoral' Symphony, the final section of 'Flos Campi' and the 'Tallis' Fantasia.

In the original score, too, the Romanza bore a quotation, 'Upon that place stood a cross, and a little below a sepulchre. Then he said, "He hath given me rest by His sorrows and life by His death",' and though the composer has now removed it from the published version, he obviously does not intend that we shall put it wholly out of our minds. How could we; for we meet the lovely themes of this movement again in the very scene of his 'Pilgrim's Progress' opera in which these words are illustrated and sung? It is clear, too, that Bunyan's book influenced the movements of this symphony that have no thematic connection with the opera.

Compared with the other symphonies, both the earlier and the later, the scoring of the fifth shows classic restraint. There are no fancy instruments; timpani alone to provide the percussion; not even a harp in this most celestial of all his compositions. There are only two horns, but the part they play in each of the four movements is particularly beautiful. To those of us who find that a certain downright clumsiness of style is part of the charm of Vaughan Williams's music, the effortless soaring architecture of this symphony can be disconcerting. It does not seem to grow like the tree-roots of the 'Pastoral' Symphony or the stone foundations of the 'Tallis' Fantasia out of our common English earth. It is an edifice of airy arches built on the other side of that river the Pilgrim was called to cross, that other side upon which all the trumpets sounded. We stand to listen, our feet upon the Delectable Mountains, not on the more familiar Cotswold Hills. This is the first and to this day the only work by Vaughan Williams that is recognisably the writing of an old man. I do not mean that it lacks vigour; very far from it. The two radiant climaxes that provide its most sublime moments have all the passion of the wedding chorus from 'Sir John — ' and are brought about with effortless ease. But this is the music of experience and wisdom, mellow and kindly. There must be, after all, much that a composer over seventy can give us, if he retains his creative vigour, that we can never obtain from the music of the young composer, however brilliant. The fact that Vaughan Williams for once was being his age may well have been the cause of the inaccurate prophecies about his future. Though I cherish and am grateful for this lovely music, yet I was not sorry that in the next two symphonies the adventurer was once more at the helm.

Horns introduce the Preludio, as the first movement is called, and, though on the surface much of this symphony seems to be meandering music, that first horn call leads as inevitably to its repetition in the last movement as the crashing first subject of the F minor Symphony leads to the fugal epilogue. A strong deep impulse, as in the superficially tranquil 'Pastoral', carries the work forward, again suggesting the analogy of the slow calm river wending its purposeful way to the sea. I must quote again the observation that William McNaught made in *The Listener* when this symphony was first performed, about one's reactions not only to this movement but to much of Vaughan Williams's music. He suggested that one went through three stages: '(a) Isn't it time something happened? (b) It is happening. (c) It has been happening all the time.' Thus in the Preludio one is led up a gentle incline, the theme gathering warmth and beginning to glow, by way of rising modulations, until one arrives suddenly into the middle of a heavenly tune, as if, as in the ballet 'Job', the clouds had rolled back to reveal the endless dance of celestial beings about God's throne. The rushing Sibelian 'development' leads eventually to the climax — Tutta Forza — whose heartbreaking intensity is achieved with such technical ease that it hardly seems to disturb the smooth surface of the music.

The Scherzo is placed second for the first time in a Vaughan

Williams symphony, assuring by its position greater weight and prominence for the slow movement which contains the heart of the symphony's matter. The words 'scherzo' and 'Vaughan Williams' found in conjunction excite a knowing anticipation. The flavours of his scherzos may be various, but there are predictable characteristics — intricacy of rhythm amd cross-rhythm, delicacy of writing for the wind. This one is marked Presto and is in fascinating contrast to the preceding golden movement, having a dark and shadowed colouring and a distinct and unexpected touch of the macabre. The feet that seem to hurry to and fro over its pages belong perhaps to the 'hobgoblins and foul fiends' of Bunyan's dread, but they keep a safe distance. Almost one can hear an echo of Mendelssohn in this flittermouse texture of woodwinds and muted strings, but Mendelssohn wrote nothing so mysterious as the swinging phrase that cuts across the pattering rhythms for the Trio. The conflict of two types of rhythm recalls the 'Concerto Accademico', though the concerto is a safe and daylight picture compared with this. The uneasy populated half-light of the Scherzo gives place to the lonely calm of the Romanza. Over a succession of peaceful chords for the strings the cor anglais plays a phrase, one that will be familiar to all who know 'The Pilgrim's Progress'. It is taken up by the strings and repeated later in the movement by the horns. Reminiscent in effect of those earlier cor anglais phrases from the slow movement of the 'London' and the first of the 'Pastoral' Symphonies, it sets the mood for this whole movement with its strange blend of longing, resignation and contentment. The music, as in the Preludio, makes a slow ascent by way of a number of themes, to a region of icy and abstracted ecstasy where the woodwind play at games in counterpoint. The return from these glittering peaks is accomplished in reverse order of themes and begins with a climax into which suddenly floods back all the warmth and colour of the symphony's early pages. Counterpoints climb upwards in contrary motion to the descending theme, prolonging the rapturous moment. In its combination of passionate longing and radiant content this passage, this whole fifth symphony, is the crowning of a long mood of benevolence

and peace that had come upon the composer after he had delivered himself of the fiery fourth. The geniality that radiated from
the 'Tudor Portraits', the affection that glowed in 'Dives and
Lazarus', the 'Serenade', the 'Household Music' shines out from
the highest plane of all in this — surely the most numinous of all
symphonies. Charity is an old-fashioned word, but the only one
that describes this present mood of the composer's.

Having delivered itself of so profound a message, of music at
once so intimate and so universal, there remains nothing for the
composer to do with his symphony but to finish it off in a burst of
high spirits. If the last movement adds little of deep consequence
it is because it follows a movement to which nothing can conceivably be added but the tribute of silence or the reaction of a
joyful noise. It is a Passacaglia — a set of variations over a 'basso
continuo'. Vaughan Williams has been accused of 'cribbing' the
theme of these variations from the Alleluia of an ancient and well-
known hymn. This he denies, pointing instead to the second
phrase of 'The First Nowell'. Be that as it may, 'Alleluia' is what
the movement triumphantly reiterates, trumpeting it to high
heaven until the horn call of the first movement cuts across the
exultant chorus with a hair-raising modulation and brings it back
to the calm of the opening pages, with a repetition of the first
subject of the symphony. The theme of this epilogue recalls the
phrase 'Nation shall not lift up a sword against nation' from 'Dona
Nobis Pacem', and again, whether or not this was conscious
reminiscence, the mood is very like that triumphant finale. The
theme returns again, subdued from its exuberance, to be the subject of the epilogue, whose lovely dying fall leads the symphony
back into silence.

There are moments in everybody's life when it is impossible to
raise the spirits to the challenge of such a symphony, and it is at
such moments that the Concerto for Oboe and Strings comes into
its own. Even with my insatiable appetite I have moods when I
would rather fly from that sublimest music. I cannot imagine a
mood or a black dog that the Oboe Concerto could not chase
from my shoulder.

Written for Leon Goossens, whose oboe, one had long believed, was bound in the end to elicit a work from Vaughan Williams, as Tertis's viola had already done, it had its first performance in 1944, the year following the Symphony in D. Amid the warm, rich summer and autumn colours of the music comprised in this chapter it lies like a sharp green windfall apple in lush grass — clean and pungent. It is gratefully unconcerned with deeper issues. The eternal verities were stated transcendently in the symphony. Written in wartime, the concerto gently affirms the smaller verities of bird-song and the unchanging country scene. The spirit is that of the 'Concerto Accademico', and the lapse of years is shown only in the richer tissue of string weaving and the more generous measure of humour. Rarely heard — perhaps because it is difficult to play — this self-contained and bracing little work bids fair to seduce me from my allegiance to that earlier small concerto.

The composer has allowed the character of his solo instrument to determine the atmosphere of his music, which is divided between a sharp and acid humour and a pastoral melancholy that remains both unsentimental and astringent. The movements — Rondo Pastorale, and Minuet and Musette — are sparing, rustic and waste no time at all. Only in the epilogue to the Finale Scherzo is richness of tone allowed for a short time to dominate. Here the oboe leads Vaughan Williams into a melody that is positively Celtic — long, plaintive and ravishing. But the oboe breaks the lovely mood that is slowly building with a harsh cadenza, its sharper tone claiming the last word, assuring us that this is not an occasion for long summer dreams or visions, but a workmanlike exercise for a virtuoso soloist and a disciplined body of strings — musician's music, not indulgence, for the listener's pleasure, in the 'concord of sweet sounds'.

'No doubt it requires a certain effort to tune oneself to the moral atmosphere implied by a fine melody', Vaughan Williams wrote in 1906 in that splendid introduction to the music of *The English Hymnal* — which should have been reprinted among his other essays, for who but a church organist, or an indefatigable seeker after his lightest word (such as myself) would ever read the

K   R.V.W.

preface to a hymn-book? It is not the 'moral atmosphere' of his own melody that disturbs me, implicit though it be in nearly all his works. It is when he comes right out into the open and challenges us with his choice of text that I find the effort to tune myself to him harder to make. No doubt this is due to that 'poverty of heart' of which, in the next sentence of that essay, he accuses us.

I am never more conscious of my own 'poverty of heart' than when I consider the texts Vaughan Williams compiled for such works as 'Dona Nobis Pacem' and its successor, the B.B.C.-commissioned 'Song of Thanksgiving' or, as it was called when it was first broadcast to all parts of the world, 'Thanksgiving for Victory'. It is my 'poverty of heart' that makes me shy of its 'moral atmosphere', that makes me faintly uncomfortable when the words from *Henry V* are declaimed by the speaker, when the Kipling poem 'Land of our Birth' is sung. Vaughan Williams does not suffer from this form of self-consciousness and his literal mind enables him to select and compile from the most unlikely sources a script that will say for him in words what his music will say in its own terms. The speaker's first words — 'O God, Thy arm was here; and not to us but to Thy arm alone ascribe we all. Take it, Lord, for it is none but Thine,' should be listened to with no accompanying picture of banners and armour on the field of Agincourt; and if Kipling's verses from *Puck of Pook's Hill*:

> *Teach us delight in simple things,*
> *And mirth that hath no bitter springs;*
> *Forgiveness free of evil done,*
> *And love to all men'neath the sun.*

are consciously naïve in language and sung here by the untrained voices of children, they do, nevertheless, sum up most of what Vaughan Williams has been saying in his music over the years. It is our 'poverty of heart' that makes us shy of them.

Perhaps we are too cynical to feel quite happy about the words of Isaiah, 'Violence shall no more be heard in thy land, wasting nor destruction within thy borders,' but this was a commissioned work for a more or less joyful occasion, and it ends on a note of responsibility and dedication that is very far from wishful thinking.

Vaughan Williams has been quoted as saying about his own work: 'Whether my music is good or bad it is always honest, and by that I mean that I could not put down on paper a line that I did not feel in every part of me.' His words can be taken as true not only of the notes of his music, but of the biblical texts and the poetry he has chosen to set them to. He has told us 'my students accuse me of turning all my lectures into sermons'. The same accusation might almost be levelled at his symphonies — at the two that preceded this 'Thanksgiving' anyway, and, as in 'Dona Nobis Pacem', the sermon in this work is inescapable.

It is not very often, except at Coronations and the Enthronisation of Archbishops, that we find Vaughan Williams writing music to order, but he seized the opportunity given him by the B.B.C.'s resources and the special intimacy of the microphone to bring together a number of musical devices that no ordinary concert planner could afford to assemble for a work lasting only fifteen minutes. This means that performances of the 'Song of Thanksgiving' are bound to be few, even given the modifications allowed for the concert hall. The special problems created by a narrator divorced from the microphone with which the original 'set-up' provided him, make 'live' performance only partly satisfactory. For this short work Vaughan Williams's original demands include a speaker, a soprano soloist who must have a ringing dramatic voice free from 'vibrato', chorus, and a separate choir of untrained children's voices. The orchestra should include double timpani, six trumpets and six clarinets.

These vast forces were not assembled at the microphone to deliver music that was startlingly original or new. It hardly requires an ear attuned to modern harmony for its appreciation. The 'Thanksgiving' was written to reach, by way of the Overseas and European Services of the B.B.C., all nations and all armies serving the world over. The music needed to be no more difficult than a Coronation anthem. Vaughan Williams wrote in that one of his many idioms that we would all, probably, choose as the most distinctively his own — the idiom of the D major Symphony, 'The Pilgrim's Progress', the robust music of the Heavenly host in 'Job'. It is supremely confident music and the work is shamelessly prodigal of magnificent tunes. They tell their own story, and it should not be necessary to understand a word of the English language to appreciate the meaning of the work.

The scenario is constructed out of Vaughan Williams's favourite sources — 'The Song of the Three Holy Children' from the Apocrypha; Chronicles; Isaiah and Shakespeare; and, an unexpected choice, Kipling's poem, which had made its appearance already in the hymn-books. There are none of the 'non sequiturs' that make 'Dona Nobis Pacem' an uncomfortable work to swallow whole. 'And not to us but to Thy arm alone ascribe we all' says the narrator, out of Shakespeare, 'take it, Lord, for it is none but Thine.' 'Thine, O Lord, is the greatness, and the power and the glory' answers the chorus, out of the Book of Chronicles, 'Thine is the victory and the majesty; for all that is in Heaven and Earth is Thine. Thine is the Kingdom.' One is unaware of any construction at all, after the initial shock of the speech after Agincourt has been absorbed. This one sentence sets the mood for the whole sober jubilation. The sermon allows no triumph to the victors. Its concern is not with the ended war, but with the reconstruction to come. It would be interesting to know if this is quite what the B.B.C. envisaged when they commissioned the work.

A terrific fanfare opens the music, echoed and repeated by the soprano. This fanfare frames and binds together the various elements in the score and all the soprano's music is based upon it. 'Blessed art Thou, O Lord, God of our fathers — ' she sings, from the song of Shadrach, Meshach and Abednego out of the burning fiery furnace, the song that is also the source of our 'Benedicite'. The organ blazes in to introduce the chorus. The chorus and the soprano sing antiphonally until the chorus dies into quietness, repeating the word 'forever', to allow the narrator to speak his words from *Henry V*. This first section ends with a fanfare call from the soprano ' — for His mercy endureth for ever.'

Over a sombre orchestral background the speaker declaims the words of Isaiah's vision: 'The spirit of the Lord God is upon me.' He enumerates the comforts he brings — 'Beauty for ashes; the oil of joy for mourning; the garment of praise for the spirit of heaviness,' and the women's voices take up and repeat each phrase, weaving their melody in and out of his words in the only triumphant justification I have ever heard of the mingling of spoken words with music.

An orchestral fanfare leads to a passage of tough and march-like rejoicing — 'Go through, go through the gates. Cast up, cast up the highway; gather out the stones; lift up an ensign for the people,' bringing back reminiscences of the splash and foam of the 'Sea' Symphony, an odd reminder of the 'Serenade to Music' as well as other curiously familiar themes impossible to pin down to any particular work — tunes that, perhaps, one always knew Vaughan Williams would 'find out' in the end. I hope it is not disrespectful to compare this rich dark music to the quality of good pre-war plum cake, a comparison that suggests itself also in the best passages of 'Dona Nobis — ', in the 'Household Music' and in 'Dives and Lazarus'. It may not be on a level with the most imaginative flights of the composer's genius as found in the symphonies, but its solidity seems to proclaim that all is really very well with English music. The toughness softens eventually into a tender downward-wending phrase, 'and thou shalt be called "Sought Out", a city not forsaken', over a rising and falling counterpoint of which the narrator declaims — 'And they shall build up the old wastes, they shall raise up the former desolation — '. He has one more speech — 'Violence shall no more be heard in thy land, wasting nor destruction within thy borders' over a pastoral quiet orchestral accompaniment, 'but thou shalt call thy walls Salvation and thy gates Praise'. The chorus takes up his words and gather themselves together for a great upward leap of joy on the final word.

This great shout sounds and feels like, and indeed easily could be, the end of the cantata; and some of us have sometimes wished it really were. But waiting, still unused, upon the platform, are that large congregation of school children and most of the six clarinets. They could hardly be there for ornament. While we are debating whether to burst into applause, a chord on the organ

announces a change of key, and with it a change of mood, colour
and atmosphere so unexpected and complete as to be positively
shocking. By now our ears are educated never to expect Vaughan
Williams to finish a work where they feel the end to be obvious,
but no amount of familiarity with his methods quite prepares
them for this. Sweetness, feminine softness even, steals in, making
one suddenly aware how unusually little of the feminine there is
in Vaughan Williams's music. The children's voices, accompanied
by those six clarinets with their ineffable chastity of tone, embark
on the first of their five verses of Kipling:

> *Land of our birth, we pledge to thee,*
> *Our love and toil in the years to be.*

On a first hearing, I admit it, I felt exceedingly sick. 'Poverty of
heart' again? I am very much afraid so.

Now, I am not anxious to join the company of 'lily-livered
critics' whom Dr Vaughan Williams derides for their failure to
enjoy the vulgar tune at the end of Beethoven's Choral Symphony; and I am satisfied that, by this date, he knows precisely the
effect he wants to produce and how to produce it. Let me, therefore, assume the garment of humility, in order to find out just why
this music makes me so uncomfortable.

The idea of reserving a special choir of children's voices to sing,
in words of one syllable, to simple everyday music, their dedication of the years to come is perhaps an obvious one. But is the
obvious necessarily wrong? Not by the standards of, for instance,
Bach or Beethoven. The sudden effect of these untrained voices
entering upon this impressive score ought to be extremely moving. Why, after I have overcome the first shocked reaction, do I
find it merely charming? The truth is that in the word 'charming'
that comes so naturally to the pen lies the root of the trouble.
Anybody who has ever tried to write a hundred or more pages
about the music of one composer will have discovered that the
English language is woefully short of adjectives. I have sat in vain,
imploring the Muses for a fresh supply, day after day. I thought I
had used them all. But I am sure that the word 'charming' never

once before suggested itself to me, and that it does not appear once in the preceding pages. Every composer appropriates to himself a little bunch of adjectives that present themselves, ready for action, whenever anybody sits down to write about him. 'Charming' is not to be found in Vaughan Williams's collection.

The hymn tune, considered on its own, is one that would be welcome in any hymn-book; simple, singable, snugly fitted to its words, a little unadventurous. It is interesting to find, by the way, that conscious artistry does not allow, in this undoubted L.M. tune, that slight pause at the end of the line that the 'unconscious artistic insight' of a congregation would, it appears, be sure to give it. As a result it goes with a swing that, after the first verse, quickly strips it of sentimentality. The doubts and misgivings, indeed, do seem to belong to the beginning of the hymn — to that modulation and the audacious switch from the sophistication of a Three Choirs Festival cantata into something like a school assembly Empire Day celebration. It is uncomfortable; but it is not impossible that Vaughan Williams foresaw our discomfiture and enjoyed it. The music gathers one into its swing. The commonplace tune reveals its potentialities, building quite naturally between the verses into a bridge passage that unites the hymn with the fanfare of the opening. Adornments grow out of the later verses, the treble voices ornamenting the tune when the men take over. Vaughan Williams has written on the subject of musical adornment, contrasting that of Bach and Haydn with Mozart's and Beethoven's. His own ornamentation is of the Bach order — an 'irrepressible exfoliation' — the unrestrained brimming over of delight as the melody develops wings and soars into the last verse's ecstatic and inevitable descant. The long and portentous preparation for this verse prepares the ear for a solemn and obvious ending here. Once again Vaughan Williams rejects it. As in 'Dona Nobis Pacem', as in the 'Pastoral' Symphony, he gives his last word to the soprano. Into the silence after the hymn her voice soars up, unaccompanied but for a distant fanfare, singing — 'The Lord shall be thy everlasting light; and the days of thy mourning shall be ended.'

CHAPTER VI

1945 - 1956

Symphony in E minor : The Pilgrim's Progress :
Oxford Elegy : Sinfonia Antartica : Coronation
Music : Tuba Concerto : Hodie : Symphony in
D minor

'You never attempt anything you cannot achieve', said Vaughan Williams to the composer and critic Cecil Gray, after some words of appreciation of an opera of Gray's he had been hearing. Gray took these words to heart, not as a commendation, but as a searching criticism of his work, coming, as it did, from that particular source. Vaughan Williams, in putting his finger on Cecil Gray's weakness, revealed his own strength.

I wonder what would have become of 'that foolish young man Ralph Vaughan Williams' of 'Aunt Etty's' letter, written, I suppose, more than fifty years ago, if he had been content to confine his attempts at composition to what he felt he could achieve. 'Unteachable' in youth, as he admits himself to have been; incorrigible in age; he confesses, 'I have learnt almost entirely what I have learnt by trying it on the dog.' He could not study. S. P. Waddington, a musician he admired, was critical, 'You try to run before you can walk.' Vaughan Williams admitted the justice of this accusation, but obstinately continued to learn chiefly by his own errors. If he had not, we may well suspect, with Aunt Etty, that he might have broken his heart in early youth.

The young man who set out, with little success behind him to bolster up his confidence, to write the first fully choral symphony ever composed; who withdrew and rewrote his 'London' Symphony after performance and publication, was not attempting only what he knew he could achieve. The experienced musician of seventy, respected and revered by all his fellow-musicians, even by those who do not like his music, might be expected to have settled down to the composition of music well within his enormous technical range. But all the evidence is to the contrary. Between the ages of seventy and eighty he took enormous risks and caused some headshaking even among his admirers. Can he have been quite confident of achievement in writing a work for harmonica (which I would still prefer to call the 'mouth-organ') and orchestra; or the rarely successful combination of speaker and orchestra — much more elaborate in his 'Oxford Elegy' than in the short episodes in the 'Song of Thanksgiving'? Then there is the 'Sinfonia Antartica'. How some musicians must have shuddered at the project of a symphony with an avowed programme, inextricably tied to utterly non-musical matters and using for some of its main themes music composed for the sound-track of a film! I love to picture the shades of some of his distinguished teachers puzzling over that monumentally-sized score. He was content, also, to allow his 'Pilgrim's Progress' opera to be put on the stage with all its imperfections on its head — imperfections of which he must have been perfectly aware. It had been awaited long and rumoured given up and shelved; but it contained some of his loveliest music — music of a kind that, one cannot help guessing, he himself prefers to much of the music of his greater works. He took the risk and tried it on the dog. Speaking for the dog, I am grateful.

The Symphony in E minor brought to an end, with a shattering roar, the composer's ten-year mood of loving-kindness. With its arrival it became immediately clear that something very odd indeed had happened to the British musical public. Here was a symphony that began as fiercely as the fiery F minor, and that, continuing through movements that grew progressively more unfriendly, ended up in as lone and drear a region of the soul as any composer at any date has ever explored. Yet this symphony took an immediate hold on the public imagination and has appeared in the concert lists with a regularity not even equalled by its predecessor at the height of its war-time emotional triumph. Four or five times a year, in London alone, the E minor Symphony seems to turn up, and I have never attended a concert hall where it was to be played that was not almost full.

Of course, Vaughan Williams has been among us long enough to have outlived the unpopularity and neglect that are the young and middle-aged composer's usual lot. To the English great age seems to be a virtue in itself, and he has become an institution. His new works are looked forward to, these days, with curiosity, even by people who do not intend ever to listen to them. Yet I would not have expected the many new friends the D major Symphony made for his music to have taken the E minor quite so readily to their hearts.

I was exhilarated and puzzled by the new work, and delighted to be puzzled. It took me longer to discover the beauty of the long, nearly inaudible Epilogue than it had taken me, six years earlier, to settle down happily with the Symphony in F minor, whose idiom was then quite strange to me.

We are not a nation ready to try new things. When a new piece of music is played in the second half of the Prom, and there is no Tchaikovsky or Beethoven to come after and keep the public in their seats, there will always be many people who will walk out in the middle of a movement — a discourtesy they would not dream of perpetrating if the composer were a dead one, even if they did not happen to like his music. Yet, in spite of ourselves, we are gradually growing acclimatised to the sort of sounds that make up this symphony. For this improvement we have to thank the films and the B.B.C. The very people who made their noisy exit during the quieter moments of the 'Antartica' at a recent Prom have probably commented favourably at some time on the excellence of a film score by Vaughan Williams, or some younger, and therefore to them, by definition, more 'modern' composer. Film music is swallowed as painlessly as music for the ballet. Nobody objects to or even notices its discordance so long as one of the other senses is kept fully occupied. Our children ought to have no difficulty at all in listening to the music of their own contemporaries, for the B.B.C.'s Children's Hour, with great imagination, has for many years been using such things as Walton's Symphony and Vaughan Williams's F minor to make their admirable thrillers more thrilling still. The new symphony was pressed into service the moment it was recorded to illustrate some fascinating serial about dark doings in the African jungle. This may not be exactly the treatment the composer envisaged for his symphonies when he composed them, but I think he should welcome it, for it is done with affection and may win him a worthwhile audience. Anyway, for whatever reason, I have not seen anyone making their exit during the Symphony in E minor.

This symphony — and this is why I am surprised that its popularity is so great — seems to reverse the emotional pattern of the F minor. The earlier work began in anger and bitterness, but ended with a devil-may-care exhilaration. It left the listener exhausted but satisfied. The new symphony, beginning with a movement of exuberant high spirits, introducing later the one broad lyrical passage the work contains, progresses through gathering darkness to a chilling and desolate Epilogue which is long, and, because of its extreme quiet, is very difficult to concentrate on in a large concert hall. I can think of no other music that so completely reverses the natural process; that begins so positively and ends so inconclusively.

The curious tone of the composer's own notes to the first performance — 'oddly derisive' Hubert Foss called them — is scarcely helpful. Either he is unwilling to commit his deeper thoughts to paper and disguises them behind a mask of jocularity, or else his own impression of the symphony is utterly different from that conveyed to his hearers. But even he dries up and can find nothing to say about the Epilogue. He is even evasive about the dates of composition — 'This symphony was begun probably about 1944 and finished in 1947. It is scored for full orchestra including saxophone. Each of the first three movements has its tail attached to the head of its neighbour.' The symphony makes larger demands upon the orchestra than the previous D major. Triangle, side drum, bass drum, cymbals, xylophone, and, if possible, two harps,

are required. The tenor saxophone plays a part of great prominence.

The opening crash and rush of the E minor has less of bitterness
and more of the elemental in it than the F minor. Frank Howes
described the earlier symphony as 'an edifice of steel and concrete',
but it is the elements that rule in the E minor, and one can almost
catch a salt tang of sea air borne in from the first of all his symphonies in the E minor's early pages. In later movements the
elemental violence suggests that the composer's mind might have
been dwelling on the possibilities of nuclear fission, but, in spite
of the insistence of some of his critics, he has stood firm in his
refusal to give countenance to any such idea. The initial fury of the
opening bars gives place to a jovial syncopated dance rhythm,
kindly in its elephantine way. I have heard this likened to 'The
Sorcerer's Apprentice', but it seems to me to be more nearly allied
to Holst's 'Uranus'. This movement from Holst's most popular
work at its first rehearsal set the char-ladies dancing as they swept
the aisles of the Queen's Hall. I should hate to listen to the first
movement of the E minor Symphony standing in the Prom, for,
inevitably, I should be dancing like them. A new theme is introduced 'cantabile' on the strings, a theme that, on its first appearance, seems to have but little lyrical attraction. This tune is repeated 'very loud' on the brass, 'and this', goes on the composer,
'brings us to what I believe the professional annotator would call
the "reprise in due course". As a matter of fact this reprise is only
hinted at, just enough to show that this is a symphony not a
symphonic poem. But I am not sure that the "due course" is well
and truly followed when we find the tune . . . played for yet a
third time (this time in E major) quietly by the strings accompanied by harp chords.' At this second repetition the tune emerges,
after one of Vaughan Williams's most glorious modulations, as a
full rounded lyrical melody, 'tranquillo', like a full-sailed ship
running before a favouring breeze. For a few moments we are
allowed to enjoy this, one of the composer's greatest tunes, and
then, for this romantic mood can hardly be tolerated longer in a
symphony of this temper, he subtly hands it over to the tenor

saxophone, whose associations, as much as its unexpected
tones in a symphonic context, strip away every trace of sweetness
and romance and prepare us for the re-entry of the crashing opening theme and the rigorous climate of the slow movement. 'To
make an end', says the programme-note, 'and just to show that
after all the movement is in E minor, there is an enlargement of
the opening bar.'

It so happened that this symphony and the film *Scott of the
Antarctic* came out at about the same time. In actual fact the symphony had been written before the film had been projected, and
there is no connection between this slow movement and the great
Antarctic continent which it so vividly calls to my mind. I doubt
even if Ealing Studios chose Vaughan Williams for his ability to
depict the waste places of the earth, but rather, I suspect, because
he can write so well a sort of heroic music that can share Elgar's
favourite direction 'nobilmente' while at the same time remaining
plainer and more English. But how Antarctic is the desolation of
this movement, with its malignant three-note figure that persists,
now quiet, now swelling to fortissimo and dying again, on the
trumpets and percussion! It is a colder picture than any he drew
in the later 'Antartica', perhaps because it is not concerned with
the solid landscape of the world, however remote, but the more
desolating possibilities of the human mind. Early in the movement the strings, in parallel motion, draw a sketch for the material
of the Epilogue. 'The trumpets start, almost inaudibly, but they
keep hammering away at their figure for over forty bars getting
louder and louder.' When their sound has died away a solo cor
anglais bridges the gap into the Scherzo.

This movement bears the closest resemblance to the methods
and style of the F minor Symphony. A grim humour is allowed a
good deal of play, particularly in the passage for the saxophone,
but it is a rackety movement, with no respite from noise, and none
of the charm that flickers through the Scherzos of the five earlier
symphonies. The charm, it seems, has been reserved for the programme notes, from which I cannot resist the temptation to quote
copiously. 'This may possibly be described as fugal in texture but

not in structure,' writes Vaughan Williams. 'The principal subject does not appear at the beginning. Various instruments make bad shots at it. . . . An episodical tune is played by the saxophone and is repeated loud by the full orchestra. . . . (Constant Lambert tells us that the only thing to do with a folk-tune is to play it soft and repeat it loud. This is not a folk-tune, but the same difficulty seems to crop up.) When the episode is over the woodwind experiment as to how the fugue subject will sound upside down, but the brass are angry and insist on playing it the right way up, so for a bit the two go on together and to the delight of everyone including the composer the two versions fit, so there is nothing to do now but to continue, getting more and more excited till the episode tune comes back very loud and twice as slow. Then once more we hear the subject softly upside down and the bass clarinet leads the way into the last movement.' The abrupt termination of this grim frolic, as if a balloon had suddenly been pricked, is a desolate moment — 'not with a bang but a whimper' — and the descending bass clarinet phrases lead eerily into the uneasy pianissimo of the long Epilogue.

Those who like to endue Vaughan Williams with a gift for prophecy have been silent over this symphony and this Epilogue, though I did once hear no less a person than Sir Adrian Boult suggest in a broadcast that perhaps this unique movement might represent the earth after an atomic war. The appearance of these pages of the score, with what the composer calls its 'whiffs of theme', is like a Byrd or Palestrina motet, so spaced and sparing is the counterpoint. The strings are played with the bows barely touching them, one cough is enough to shatter the tenuous spider-thread of reasoning. The weaving counterpoint is not unlike the F minor Symphony's slow movement, but that movement had a warm marching bass below its surface. Here nothing so determinate intrudes. And yet, towards the end, as the compelling mazy motion of the long chromatic phrases takes a hold upon the senses, a warmth does begin to steal in. A ray of hope shines out. The grey mist rises over the flat land and the faint light of dawn begins to grow. By the time the harp has taken its turn with the theme the score has flushed a faint gold. 'The strings', says the man who is supposed to control their destinies, 'cannot make up their minds whether to finish in E flat major or E minor. They finally decide on E minor, which is, after all, the home key.' And they bring us home into an unforeseen peacefulness on a niente chord, after which, as after the 'Pastoral' and the D major Symphonies, there is no noise more inappropriate than clapping.

Vaughan Williams has a subtle recipe of his own for anticipating criticism. There were good reasons for subtitling 'Job' not a 'ballet' but a 'Masque for Dancing'. Perhaps the reasons for calling 'The Pilgrim's Progress' not an opera but a 'Morality . . . founded upon Bunyan's allegory of the same name' were not quite so honest. In so naming it he drew attention to its shortcomings even more effectively than if he had not tried to explain them away. 'The Pilgrim's Progress' was produced in 1951 at Covent Garden and was the composer's contribution to the Festival of Britain celebrations of that summer. It was his longest and most full-scale theatrical work and, if Mozart's 'Magic Flute', which, in action, it somewhat resembles, is accepted as opera, I can see no reason why 'The Pilgrim's Progress' should escape classification under that heading.

The 'opera' (if I may call it that for the sake of brevity) hardly belongs, by any right, in this chapter at all, sandwiched uncomfortably mid-way between those two cold symphonies, the E minor and the 'Antartica'. But where else is it to go? One whole scene, virtually unchanged, comes to us from the far past of the post-Great War period, from the neighbourhood of the 'Pastoral' Symphony and the Mass. It had been performed in 1922 with chamber orchestra, under the title 'The Shepherds of the Delectable Mountains'. In 1945, when the serene D major Symphony came to comfort us, we were told of the unfinished 'Pilgrim's Progress' opera from which some of its themes were taken. So it seems likely that the scene from Act I, when the Pilgrim is relieved of his burden, must at least have been composed by then. It is hardly surprising that a work composed over a period of nearly thirty years seems a little disjointed.

The opera had been rumoured as abandoned some years before we saw it on the stage. The impression it gives is that Vaughan Williams, with no sense of urgency, had been, over the years, slowly composing music for the parts that attracted him, leaving the connecting links and the bits he liked less to be filled in in a rush in time for production. This does not seem at all like Vaughan Williams's usual practice, but what else can one deduce from a score that contains some of the most glorious music he ever wrote, side by side with passages that are not only ineffective from the theatrical point of view, but are musically positively dull? Could it be that the Festival committee hurried him into delivering up this work before he was absolutely satisfied with it?

The libretto is responsible for quite half the trouble, but Dr Vaughan Williams is responsible for the libretto and must therefore take all the blame. Bunyan's story has no lack of colourful incident, conflict and action. The germ is there for as dramatic an opera as one could wish to hear. Vaughan Williams seems to have been inspired only by the holy passages and the pastoral interludes, and he has made some of these more static than they need have been. The costumes, the production, even more, the settings, were partly responsible for an atmosphere of Church Pageant that hung oddly in the air of Covent Garden when these scenes were being played. When the music is at its most rapturously seductive the Pilgrim is, for the most part, occupied in putting on or taking off symbolical garments, surrounded by youths and chaste maidens in robes reminiscent of a Deaconess's retreat. And is it not a little sad that the Pilgrim (who, presumably, was of Bunyan's puritan and Low Church turn of mind) should cross the river to find himself received into a Heaven so be-vestmented and obviously Anglo-Catholic? These were faults in the production; but who would have thought that the creator of Satan in 'Job' would invent so mild an Apollyon; that the composer of the drear Epilogue of the symphony last discussed could not make the Valley of the Shadow of Death a place of more awful horror; that the man who made 'Sir John in Love' and 'Five Tudor Portraits' so bursting with robust life could not paint the fleshly attractions of Vanity Fair in more alluring colours? These scenes, that ought to be the most telling, for what is the Pilgrim allegory about if not the dangers of this world, are tame, and the last, Vanity Fair, almost banal. The Vanity Fair music, in fact, seems to me the least inpired that Vaughan Williams has ever laid before us. I would not mind so much about these blemishes — for, after all, in all his long career Vaughan Williams has written only too little music that I do not adore — if it were not that they exist side by side with so many precious things whose future may be jeopardised. I do not imagine 'The Pilgrim's Progress' will ever establish itself in the regular repertoire of either of our opera houses. I have lain awake at night worrying about the fate of those sublime moments and delicious details that the score contains, for, in spite of anything I may have written about this 'morality', if a good fairy were to appear and offer me a performance of any one of Vaughan Williams's works I cared to choose except the Piano Concerto, 'The Pilgrim's Progress' is the work that I would unhesitatingly order.

Consider the lovely things in it, for we have dwelt enough on its shortcomings: the majestic opening which is the hymn tune 'York', solemnly appropriate on the brass to Bunyan's story, just as it was enchantingly appropriate on the bells opening the second act of 'Hugh the Drover', leading here into a melismatic figure that is to return at the end of the opera as the Alleluia chorus among the trumpets on the Other Side: the loving music of the scene in which the Pilgrim staggers to the sepulchre to be relieved of his burden by the Shining Ones, the scene opening over the slow D major Symphony chords, the longing phrase of the cor anglais repeated, a touch of new and sensuous colour added by the harp that had been excluded from that symphony's score, the well-known music encountered again, the same, yet different, a moment of rapturous reunion. I heard this transformed, familiar music first at a rehearsal in Manchester, which the Covent Garden company were then visiting. The composer was present, allowing himself to be overruled, gently but quite firmly, by the very young, and at that time quite unknown, conductor, Leonard Hancock, whom he had chosen to conduct the opera's première.

The music never sounded quite so wonderful in Covent Garden as it did in that bare Manchester hall at eleven o'clock in the morning.

There is a fine business-like tune for the Pilgrim's hymn, 'He who would valiant be — ', and the heraldic phrase on the trumpet, played on the stage, is the leitmotif for the King's Highway upon which the Pilgrim sets out. If beauty on the scale of the 'Serenade to Music' is wanted, then nothing could be more graceful than the peaceful duet of the two Heavenly Beings — soprano and contralto — who bring, one a branch from the tree 'whose leaves are for the healing of nations', and the other, a cup of the Water of Life, as the Pilgrim lies exhausted from his encounter with Apollyon. The greatest passage in the opera is the scene in prison after Vanity Fair. To quote the composer's own précis of the scene: 'The Pilgrim, left alone in prison, at first gives way to despair. Suddenly he remembers the key of Promise. The doors fly open and he is free. The Pilgrim's Way appears before him and he sets forth again on his journey.' This is a bare statement of a scene which progresses from such black dejection to such radiant certainty. The aria is made up, chiefly, from snatches of the Psalms, beginning in the despair of 'My God, My God, look upon me. Why hast Thou forsaken me?' and rising to the confident joy of 'If I take the wings of the morning . . . even there Thy hand shall guide me and Thy right hand shall hold me'. The orchestra, beginning in angry and discordant muttering, calms into tranquillity, the Pilgrim, rising from the deadness of despair to broad 'arioso', sinks back again to the beatitude of peace, 'For Thy word is a lantern unto my feet and a light unto my path,' in one of those gentle, unspectacular Vaughan Williams phrases so closely fitted to the words that they can never again be divided. After the doors have been thrown open to reveal 'the infinite shining Heavens' and the Pilgrim has stepped out on to the King's Highway, the orchestra swells up into a long obbligato of shimmering ecstasy. A. E. F. Dickinson's saying, which I quoted earlier, that Vaughan Williams 'sees Heaven open as the door of his own home' was never more perfectly illustrated than by the end of this aria and by other episodes in 'The Pilgrim's Progress'. Noble and holy though the music may be, it is not remote. It has something of homely intimacy and sensuous attractiveness that makes his view of Heaven more desirable than the one with which we are usually presented. Most religious music paints a Heaven coldly admirable. We do not really long to be there. Even Vaughan Williams's Heaven is not, in 'Job', a place where we would be entirely at our ease. There is a severity behind those swinging tunes. The Heaven he paints in 'The Pilgrim's Progress' is delectable beyond anything the world has to offer, and he makes his listeners yearn for it with the longing he expresses in the D major Symphony's divine Romanza. Perhaps that is why the conflict in this opera is so hopelessly uneven, for, if the music of the Heavenly City is anything like that which rings out over the King's Highway, who could fail to desire to go there?

Vaughan Williams has never been one to allow the Devil all the good tunes. His policy, begun in the editing of *The English Hymnal* in 1906, of appropriating for God all the best tunes that all the ages had to offer, is carried out in his own music too. Satan, in 'Job', does very poorly for tunes compared with the hosts of Heaven. In 'The Pilgrim's Progress', however, two of the Devil's lesser agents — Mr and Madam By-Ends ('Mr By-Ends has been provided with a wife' reads the programme note) — are allowed a deliciously tuneful scene over a syncopated and infectious dance rhythm that sets the audience laughing by its sheer felicity and makes one long for the composer, once again, to get down to expressing his gift for pure melody in another light opera. This enchanting and wholly unnecessary episode, when the Pilgrim encounters this rather doubtful couple from the town of Fairspeech, is sandwiched between the verses of a song sung by a woodcutter's boy: 'He that is down need fear no fall — '. It is one of the simplest and most perfect tunes Vaughan Williams ever invented and was the one we all went away trying to remember after the performance was over; for, typically, he tantalises his audience by allowing the Pilgrim to soliloquise across the second verse and intruding the long By-Ends episode before we are per-

mitted to hear the end of the song. Having teased our ears in the
opera he made amends by allowing the tune to be published as a
separate song. For such moments as this one can forgive a few
Vanity Fairs.

'The Shepherds of the Delectable Mountains', as the second
scene of this last act is still called, is altogether another story. Lacking the full mature lyricism of the later-composed music, it has a
sweet austere atmosphere of its own, taking one, a little nostalgi-
cally, back to the dew-fresh days when musicians got up early to
chase the folk-song. It has a sharp tang of morning air that has not
blown upon us earlier in the opera, with its rich autumnal scoring.
I do not agree with the critics who wrote that this work from 1922
does not fit happily into the 1951 score. Its slight austerity, its
temperature like that of the mild 'Pastoral' Symphony, mark out
the Delectable Mountains as a region different from the lowlands
the Pilgrim has put behind him. He is near death; the shepherds
who minister to him are only half-worldly, the thinner scoring
exemplifies the rarefied air of those uplands from which the gates
of the Heavenly City can be descried. The shepherds sing in plainsong fashion, 'senza misura', the solo instruments are refreshing
after the luxuriousness of some of the earlier episodes. A bird,
represented by a soprano voice, distantly sings the Twenty-third
Psalm. The drama of the Heavenly Messenger, his arrow 'sharp-
ened with love', pierces the heart of the listener and the Pilgrim
alike, the incident moving in its understatement in a way that none
of the bigger, earlier scenes are moving. In the simplicity of this, as
in 'Riders to the Sea', Vaughan Williams shows a theatrical judgement so sound that one wonders how it could have deserted him in
the Valley of the Shadow of Death.

Amid trumpet fanfares and the sweeping Alleluias sketched for
us in the opera's prologue, the Pilgrim is received into the Heavenly
City. After a brief jubilation the curtain falls and John Bunyan,
who had introduced the opera, returns to close it; he comes forward to offer his book while the majesty of brass reminds us again
of the ancient hymn tune 'York' of the beginning, the selection of
which is as great a testimony to Vaughan Williams's genius as

any original tune, however magnificent, that he might have chosen to compose.

The 'Romance for Harmonica and Strings', written for the astonishing virtuoso of that humble instrument, Larry Adler, was heard (twice) at a Prom in the following year. It was a good-humoured occasion and everybody was delighted and gave the music a hearty encore. I was as carried away as the rest of the audience at the time and my admiration for the variety of noises the composer and the soloist manage to conjure out of that small but versatile instrument has in no way abated with time. But I have never been able, at later hearings, to recapture the excitement of that first performance, for, when all is said and done, the harmonica is, for most of us, a nauseous instrument, its piercing sickliness of tone delightful only, I should have thought, to that epicure of indiscreet sonority, Monsieur Olivier Messiaen. I have no doubt, however, that the 'Romance' will settle down happily as an annual event at the Proms, until Mr Adler is as advanced in years as Dr Vaughan Williams. I am afraid it will remain, for me, the one and only among his works that I would prefer, on the whole, not to hear.

To celebrate his eightieth birthday — 12th October, 1952 —a special concert was given in the composer's honour in a packed and cheering Festival Hall; but Vaughan Williams has always given the impression that he is happiest in the smaller and more personal gatherings where, all his life, he has made music among his friends and neighbours. His own musical organisation at Leith Hill, Dorking, honoured his birthday with a performance of 'An Oxford Elegy' for speaker, small chorus and small orchestra. The speaker on that occasion was C. Day Lewis, Professor of Poetry in the University of Oxford. The elegy had already been given its first performance at Queen's College, Oxford, earlier in the year, but it was not broadcast until June of the Coronation year, and its first London performance was not until May, 1954, when Robert Speaight read the words. At the age of eighty it seems as if, almost deliberately, Vaughan Williams had chosen to compose a work that reaches back to the earliest of his moods and styles, a work illustrating with unique clarity that unity and steadfastness of vision that shines like a beam of light straight through the fantastic variety of his writings of the past fifty years. Most composers abandon one style in favour of another and another as the years go past, but that has not been Vaughan Williams's way. He has not broken with his past at any point and is as likely now to offer us some maturer example of the kind of music he was writing in the Housman songs or 'Riders to the Sea' as of continuing on the lines of the F minor and E minor Symphonies and the 'Landscape' movement of his next symphony, the 'Antartica'. The choice of text and the simple Englishness of some of the melody links the elegy far back with the Rossetti and Stevenson songs of the first decade of the century. The young Vaughan Williams who chose Rossetti's words:

> far as the eye can pass
> Are golden kingcup-fields with silver edge
> Where the cow-parsley skirts the hawthorn hedge.
> 'Tis visible silence, still as the hour-glass

to set to an immortal song in 1903, might equally well have chosen:

> Pale pink convolvulus in tendrils creep;
> And air-swept lindens yield
> Their scent, and rustle down their perfumed showers
> Of bloom on the bent grass where I am laid.

The words are by Matthew Arnold, adapted from the 'Scholar Gipsy' and from 'Thyrsis'. The speaker declaims the long verses and the music for the chorus and small orchestra surround and accompany him. Reason insists that Vaughan Williams was here attempting the impossible, that speech and music can never blend, at any rate in a large concert hall and in so long a work, that one's concentration can never encompass both together. Remembering that first broadcast, with the speaker close to the microphone, quietly reading the words to one's inner ear, I am not so sure. Probably a recording is the only answer to the problem, for with an intimate knowledge of both the music and the poetry, one might hope in the end to attain a state of relaxation sufficient to permit the elegy freely to 'creep in our ears'.

'An Oxford Elegy' is not one of Vaughan Williams's prophetic works, wrested out of him by the compulsion of his genius and the times it had to grow in, but one of the many quiet writings dropped by the wayside, written because it gave him pleasure to write it; written, as so many, to celebrate his enduring delight in the English country scene; no easier to classify than the 'Serenade to Music' and almost equally compounded of pure harmoniousness. And how sad it is! Filled to the brim with the melancholy that used to shadow the early song-cycles; but made sweet and pleasurable by the soft balance of tone from the small orchestra, from the chorus who now hum, now sing, as in 'Flos Campi', on a vowel-sound, now echo the speaker's words and, at last, triumphantly, have one long lovely passage all to themselves:

> Soon will the high Midsummer pomps come on,
>   Soon will the musk-carnations break and swell,
> Soon shall we have gold-dusted snapdragon,
>   Sweet-William with his homely cottage-smell,
> And stocks in fragrant blow;
>   Roses that down the alleys shine afar,
> And open, jasmine-muffled lattices,
>   And groups under the dreaming garden-trees,
> And the full moon, and the white evening star.

'An Oxford Elegy' is not all summer beauty; it has its wintry moments, earlier, with the women's voices undulating behind the speaker's declamation in an anticipation of the wind of the Antarctic; and it ends with a tune which is all spring, all hope, which gathers into four short lines of verse all the freshness of 1903 with the mastery of fifty years of work and living, in an English tune of piercing sweetness:

> I wandered till I died.
> Roam on! the light we sought is shining still.
> Our tree yet crowns the hill.
> Our scholar travels still the loved hillside.

'Our scholar travels still the loved hillside.' Indeed he does, a scholar always, to our great profit and satisfaction; but it was not the Oxfordshire landscape that had principally engaged his mind in the years between *Scott of the Antarctic*, one of the most remarkable of film-scores ever composed, and the year that the 'Sinfonia Antartica' had its first performance on a bleak and foggy winter night in Manchester — 14th January, 1953.

To an explorer of the unknown of Vaughan Williams's long experience a journey to the Poles or, perhaps, to the summit of Mount Everest, must make as strong an appeal as the Pilgrim's journey from the City of Destruction to Mount Zion. There were people who found it a matter for wonder that he should wish to compose a symphony upon the theme of Captain Scott's tragic expedition, avowedly inspired by the music he had written for that film. I did not find it surprising.

Up till this moment, with scant success, I fear, I have tried to maintain a decent detachment, to meet the music that came under review with cold sanity. There have been times when the struggle was unequal. Reaching the 'Antartica' I give it up for good. For I know exactly why this music had to be written. I understand as well as anyone the irresistible fascination that must at some time have gripped the composer to compel him to make, from the material of a film-score, so monumental and unusual a work.

I have already admitted that if I were to be banished to a desert island with the eight gramophone records which the B.B.C. allows its castaways, these records would be of music by Vaughan Williams. If it were books with which I were to be marooned my first choices would be Scott's *Voyage of the Discovery* and *Last Expedition* and Apsley Cherry-Garrard's great book, *The Worst Journey in the World*. Since I discovered them I have read them yearly with never-diminished excitement and affection, and, besides them, every bit of Antarctic literature that I can lay my hands on. I can no more explain the sway over my imagination held by that particular journey, that group of men, that white unfriendly continent, than I can explain why certain modal cadences and a continual hesitation between the major and minor which characterise Vaughan Williams's style should make his music more beautiful to my ears than any other composer's. I have travelled every step of the way in my imagination up the Beardmore Glacier, across the plateau to the Pole and back again to the final blizzard on the Barrier with Scott and Wilson and Bowers, with Oates and Evans, and now — in a different revelation — with Vaughan Williams. Consequently it is not reasonable to expect me to be sane about the 'Sinfonia Antartica'.

That Vaughan Williams was gripped also by this inexplicable lure the Polar wastes exert is evident from his powerfully evocative music, particularly in the stark third movement; and his ability to soak in atmosphere by reading is startlingly illustrated by the fact that, as the story goes, he composed every note of his film-score before he had been able to see a single foot of film. He worked to written descriptions and minute timings and it is said that when music and film were at last brought together, hardly a note had to be altered. By then the fascination of the land-scape and the story had so taken hold of him that he was itching to begin his symphony even before the film had been publicly shown.

Vaughan Williams has been definite in his permission to us to think of this as 'programme' music. His notes, written for that first performance by the Hallé Orchestra, contain none of the evasions that were made about the 'London' Symphony. He does not insist — 'Those who wish may take it as representing whales' he says of a passage in the Scherzo, but we may take it that it is whales for him. He has, moreover, given, in his quotation placed over the movements of the 'Sinfonia', a picture of the emotions the story arouses in him:

> To suffer woes which hope thinks infinite,
> To forgive wrongs darker than death or night,
> To defy power that seems omnipotent,
> Neither to change, nor falter, nor repent;
> This is to be
> Good, great and joyous, beautiful and free,
> This is alone life, joy, empire and victory.

words by Shelley, which he had set earlier as one of a group of unison songs 'To be sung in time of war', and a quotation from Donne:

> *Love, all alike, no season knows, nor clime,*
> *Nor hours, days, months, which are the rags of time.*

One is grateful for these revelations of his thought, but these quotations, which are a comfort to audiences who have been beaten into a submissive belief that programme music is somehow deplorable, have proved themselves a menace. The B.B.C. has, on several occasions, permitted their announcer to read them aloud between the movements. More horrifying still, in a broadcast overseas, Sir John Barbirolli himself delivered them, with comments. The composer has obviously given his blessing to this intolerable practice, for in the newest recording of the work, the one personally supervised by himself, Sir John Gielgud is dragged in to read them. That he reads them as beautifully as anybody could does nothing to convince me that the composer is right. The intrusion of a human voice upon this elemental music could not have a more disastrous effect!

The orchestra is vast and very impressive to see assembled on the platform, although what can be seen is by no means the whole story. Hidden away is a choir of women's voices and a wind machine. It would be simpler to list the instruments that do not appear in the score, a score of such dimensions that a critic, speaking about the 'Sinfonia' in a broadcast before its first performance, said he had been afraid he might have to take off his front door to admit it to his house for study! Besides the vibraphone and the xylophone demanded, there are parts for three keyboard instruments — celesta, piano and organ. These enormous forces are used so sparingly that there does not seem to be one instrument that could be sacrificed without its absence being fatal to the total effect. The unusual instruments are used, now with discretion, as, for instance, the piano's dry little 'ostinato' in the Epilogue; now with marvellous indiscretion, like the horrific organ episode in the third movement — a fortissimo that shakes the soul and must make the ghost of Berlioz sick with envy.

The Prelude leads straight off with its principal theme. 'This theme is used as a whole or in part throughout the work,' says Vaughan Williams in his notes. No other symphony I know, except that of E. J. Moeran, opens thus, utterly without preamble. It is a theme that must be remembered by anybody who saw *Scott of the Antarctic*, plodding upwards determinedly, heavy with the weight of dragged and laden sledges. It emerges at the summit into a passage of brittle glitter — 'a few Antarctic shimmerings' the composer describes it. At intervals throughout this score he uses his glockenspiel, xylophone, vibraphone, celesta and harp to fill the air uncannily with tingling vibration, etching an impression of prismatic light, of circular rainbows, of parhelia, and all the phenomena produced by interaction of sun and ice that give their colour to a world of white. Another of the few themes that come straight out of the film-score follows. A disembodied soprano voice soars eerily over a background of the moaning of women's voices, and the weird rise and fall of the wind machine. No instrument conceivable could produce a sound so desolate, so inhuman, as that human voice, expressing as no words ever could the mysterious call that lures men to go out to the uncharted wastes of the earth and, if necessary, to die there. It is electrifying to hear this voice floating over the vast silent and motionless orchestra, its barely audible accompaniment also hidden from sight. 'This is followed', Vaughan Williams's notes continue, 'by other themes of minor importance which lead to a theme accompanied by deep bells which was supposed, in the film, to be "menacing".' This theme also reappears later in the work. The soprano theme is repeated here, and there is a soft fanfare, suggestive, though I fear I am giving too 'material' an interpretation even for this music, of the entrance on this desolate landscape of human figures. A certain bustling activity in the following bars bears out this impression. The coda is built up 'largely on the opening theme'.

> *There go the ships*
> *And there is that Leviathan*
> *Whom thou hast made to take his pastime therein.*

This quotation from the 104th Psalm, over the Scherzo which follows, introduces that theme, in which, if we wish, we are permitted to imagine whales. It is an endearing picture, the composer obviously holding these largest of created beings in affectionate esteem. 'The next section', goes on the programme note, 'would, I suppose, be called by the official analyst, the "trio". Its tune was used in the film to suggest penguins.' There, indeed, it did most ably accompany the curious bouncing motion of a penguin out of water, in an amusing episode. I am not sure how well this part of the symphony would stand alone as music, if one did not know the scenario on which it is based.

Over the next movement, 'Landscape', Vaughan Williams set a quotation from Coleridge:

> *Ye Icefalls! Ye that from the mountain's brow*
> *Adown enormous ravines slope amain —*
> *Torrents, methinks, that heard a mighty voice,*
> *And stopped at once amid their maddest plunge.*
> *Motionless torrents! Silent cataracts!*

and the static, frozen majesty the poem describes has been caught in music that is solid as a crag of ice. There is a photograph in *Scott's Last Expedition* entitled 'The Ramparts of Erebus', a picture of sheer fissured white crags against a black sky, towering above an ant-like human figure with a sledge; and it is this picture that the music recalls to me. 'The music here is chiefly atmospheric', writes the composer, mildly describing what he has depicted in music quite stark in its lonely terror. It builds slowly like the panorama of a glacier, gradually unfolding to the peak where the brass of the orchestra thunders up to meet the terrifying entry of the organ. This overwhelming passage makes, in its ferocity, the Coleridge verses seem a wordy elaboration, and I wish Vaughan Williams had simply put over his music Scott's great cry from the Polar diary — 'Great God, this is an awful place!' This intimidating movement melts without a break into the gentle Intermezzo by way of the Donne quotation and some chords on the harp. The icy landscape is suffused with loving warmth. The effect of this modulation and change of colour is comparable with and not unlike the second repetition of the great lyrical tune in the first movement of the E minor Symphony. Over the harp notes, more intimate than that great melody, the oboe plays a theme entirely characteristic of the composer, swinging between major and minor, bringing from another hemisphere its breath of Cotswold air, its lingering reminiscence of 'The Lark Ascending', the melody of the third fiddler from the 'Old King Cole' ballet, the 'Pastoral' Symphony, even of 'Hugh the Drover'. Gloucestershire is conjured out of the Antarctic blizzard — 'Love, all alike, no season knows, nor clime — '. Scott and his companions perished in 1912, the period when Vaughan Williams was writing his most pastoral and English music. Is it accidental that this melody carries so strong a flavour of the kind of tune he was writing then? This warm consoling movement nestles, against all reason, snugly between the icy one that precedes it, and the unsentimental toughness of the Epilogue. Its meaning is plain. In the film, when the explorers lay dying in their tent, eleven miles from safety, they were visited by visions, in a series of flashbacks, of their homes and wives. The device was only partially successful. With entire success in the 'Sinfonia Antartica' Vaughan Williams leads us to think on the same subject. After another, quicker, theme of equal pastoral enchantment the menacing bell passage is repeated, and after it 'some very soft music connected in the film with the death of Oates'.

The Epilogue is introduced by a strong energetic march tune, derived from the germinal theme of the opening, its rough movement dispelling the lingering warmth of the Intermezzo, for though men may die exploration goes on. Those who await a noble patriotic tune to round off the heroic story will be disappointed. Vaughan Williams, who can write such tunes so well, rarely chooses to do so. He neither uses here nor provides an alternative for the broad melody that ended the film and illustrated the epitaph chosen for the explorer's memorial — 'To strive, to seek, to find and not to yield'. Vaughan Williams does not set this quotation over his Epilogue, but selects a drier one from Scott: 'We took risks, we knew we took them, things have come out against us, therefore we have no cause for complaint,' the first two phrases of which sentence could be applied to many a hazard of the composer's own, this one no less than any. After the march, 'the bell passage comes in again, suddenly very soft. The voices are heard and the trumpet flourish, first loud then soft.' The slow climbing theme of the opening is recapitulated in full, carrying, perhaps, the suggestion that such journeys will continue to be made so long as man remains. But in the end it is the Antarctic that conquers, as perhaps, in our hearts, we wish it always should. The symphony ends with the unearthly siren voice calling through the wind from the midst of the desolate continent, mocking the feeble efforts of man to pluck out the heart of its mystery. 'The music', says the composer, 'dies down to nothing, except for the voices and the Antarctic wind.'

The 'Sinfonia Antartica' is not only music on a grand symphonic scale, it is also the most unexpected and moving of all the memorials that have been dedicated to Scott and his companions on the Polar Journey. My own twice-precious copy of the score lives, not among the music on my shelves, but in the section of my bookcase that holds the books on the Antarctic — beside the *Last Expedition* and *The Worst Journey in the World*.

The year of the 'Antartica' — 1953 — was also the year of Queen Elizabeth's Coronation, and Vaughan Williams composed two of the new items in that long list of music from all periods of our history. They were utterly different, but both unmistakably his own. Yet, strangely enough, it was the two extracts from his Mass in G Minor of 1922, the Credo and the Sanctus, that sounded the most modern of all the compositions we heard that day, in their simple, polyphonic austerity. It was not his turn to provide the Te Deum, nevertheless he contrived to make the most joyful noise in the whole ceremony. He made, for the first time at any Coronation, an opportunity for the congregation in the Abbey, as well as the thousands listening outside in the rain, to burst their lungs in singing and make their contribution to the jubilations of the day. He chose, for his purpose, a hymn that everybody would know, the 'Old Hundredth' — 'All People that on Earth do Dwell' — and set it about with fanfares that rang round the Abbey roof as the fanfares of his 1937 Te Deum had rung for George VI. Not all the verses were for general singing; in the third verse a splendid trumpet descant soared above the choir; in the fourth the descant was maintained by the boys, while the tenors took over the tune.

The little motet, 'O taste and see how gracious the Lord is — ', written for the moment of the Queen's Communion, was the one small, personal and feminine item in the great service, the one that had obviously been composed because it was a young Queen who was being crowned. Drifting down like manna from Heaven upon a solo treble voice, joined later by the other voices, pale and translucent as a consecrated wafer, it brought a sudden reminiscence of the Shepherd Boy and his enchanting song out of 'The Pilgrim's Progress'. Lasting a bare minute, quiet and unaccompanied, it was, nevertheless, one of the most impressive moments in the whole ceremony.

Since his eightieth birthday Vaughan Williams's pen has not ceased to eat up music-paper at its accustomed rate — if anything, indeed, his demands for it seem to have increased. Besides his music for the Coronation ceremony he contributed a beautiful grave part-song — 'Silence and Music' — with words by Ursula Wood, to the collection composed, at that time, by English musicians, *A Garland for the Queen*. At the same time, a masque, 'The Bridal Day', also by Ursula Wood, with music by Vaughan Williams, founded on Spenser's *Epithalamium*, was performed on television, the composer thereby letting us know that he was properly up to date with the youngest and least developed of the arts. Vaughan Williams has not often written especially for broadcasting, but in this year, also, he composed a score for the B.B.C.'s West Region, for their serial play 'The Mayor of Casterbridge', dramatised from Thomas Hardy's novel. Out of this, which only the West of England was privileged to hear, was rescued, for the concert-goer, one short and eloquent meditation, 'Prelude on an old Carol Tune', scored with affection and warmth. The first performance of this, outside the studio, was conducted by the composer at short notice in the King's Lynn Festival of 1953.

Vaughan Williams's 'Harmonica Romance', mentioned earlier in this chapter, proved to be the starting point of a positive flood of mouth-organ concertos and other pieces by composers of distinction that shows little sign of abating. Whether the tuba, from the opposite end of the musical spectrum, in his promotion of it to soloist from its humble necessary existence in the orchestra's back row, will start another fashion remains to be seen.

His Concerto for Bass Tuba, believed to be the first of its kind, had its first performance at the Festival Hall on 13th June, 1954. This concerto was not written with any particular virtuoso performer in mind, but written simply out of the composer's affection for the voice of this comical instrument. One prediction only could safely be made about the music to be played for the first time that evening — that he would use his elephantine protagonist to create something of enduring beauty, whatever boisterous fun he might enjoy with it by the way. He would be the last person in the world to bring a musical instrument out of its decent obscurity only to make it a figure of fun. He has turned his hand, in recent years, to the creating of sonorities as strange as any modern composer has ever invented, but the results have never been other than or less than music. In his central movement — Romance — our expectation of beauty was fulfilled.

Vaughan Williams's own programme note is so sparing that it can be quoted here in full : 'The form of this concerto is nearer to the Bach form than that of the Viennese school (Mozart and Beethoven) though the first and last movements finish up with an elaborate cadenza which allies the Concerto to the Mozart-Beethoven form. The music is fairly simple and obvious and can probably be listened to without much previous explanation. The orchestration is that of the so-called Theatre Orchestra consisting of woodwind, two each of horns, trumpets and trombones, timpani, percussion and strings.'

'Simple and obvious' to listen to, perhaps, but not quite so simple to play, for rarely can the tuba have been called upon to display so much agility, and that without the covering sounds of other instruments in a tutti. The cadenzas call for formidable concentration and delicate precision. The Prelude movement with its infinity of cross-rhythmic interest, of a kind to be found in any Vaughan Williams scherzo, recreates with a pleasanter humour something of the atmosphere of Vanity Fair; the final Rondo alla Tedesca is biting and forthright, and both movements end unerringly, as do all the composer's works since the days of the 'Sea' Symphony and 'Hugh the Drover', a few moments sooner than the listener would expect or wish — a discipline that was the more noticeable at this concert because the new work followed Elgar's lovely Violin Concerto, uncut and vastly too expansive, however we may love it, for our present-day impatience. The central movement of the Tuba Concerto, a jewel in its setting, could have been twice as long to everyone's delight. The strings lead the tuba into as flowing, shapely and beautiful a pastoral melody as Vaughan Williams has ever conjured out of the air around him — mellow as autumn and fresh as spring all in one tune, with his major – minor hesitations, timeless as some of his very greatest writings are. In his concluding speech, the chairman of the orchestra referred to Dr Vaughan Williams as 'our youngest composer', and if the date of his birth had not been recorded on the programme it is very possible that a visiting foreigner or even a native of this island, ignorant as I had been only fourteen years ago, might have taken the statement for literal truth. For the evidence of the music is of exuberant and lyrical delight, of a spring of unending melody and rhythmic invention, bubbling as irrepressibly as ever it did back in those days when the composer filled his first two symphonies full of more tunes than any respectable symphony can possibly contain.

With the publication of 'Hodie' — 'This Day' — and its performance in Worcester Cathedral at the Three Choirs Festival of 1954 Vaughan Williams gave us his first large-scale choral work since the short 'Song of Thanksgiving' with which he celebrated the end of the war.

M

R.V.W.

'Hodie' had its first hearing in the vast and rather dwarfing cathedral on a damp and chill September evening at the end of a wet cold summer. My memory of the morning rehearsal is of sunshine and warmth, which must have been supplied by the bright splashes of brass and the variety of colourful percussion, for, going out of the cathedral into the close at lunchtime, it was surprising to discover that the skies were still overcast and the rain still falling straight and cold.

Christmas is the occasion for 'Hodie' — the title is taken from the Vespers for Christmas Day, 'Hodie Christus natus est' — and Christmas is an occasion that demands music. Vaughan Williams filled a gap and supplied a need with this big work that lasts only five minutes short of an hour. Up till now the only big Christmas works we have had are the 'Messiah' and Bach's 'Christmas Oratorio', with the doubtful occasional addition of Berlioz's 'Childhood of Christ', which is not really a Christmas work at all. For the rest of the season we have to be content with carols — among them some of the loveliest tunes in the world, and yearly added to by living composers and by discoveries out of the past — but they are not quite the substantial musical fare we need to balance our more earthly celebrations. A real jubilation, a paean of praise, has been lacking for centuries. 'Hodie' vigorously supplies the lack and, I predict, will be taken up by choral societies all over the country and become in the end almost as popular as Handel's famous Christmas music. A great many of the instruments in the big orchestra are cued and may be omitted, as is usual in Vaughan Williams's works, so as to make the cantata accessible to choirs and orchestras with small resources; but the barbaric splendour of this music depends upon the lavishness of the scoring, and a performance of 'Hodie' in which the exotic elements had been reduced to their bare minimum would hardly be a performance of 'Hodie' at all.

This is not Vaughan Williams's only Christmas music. In the early 1920's he published a 'Fantasia on Christmas Carols' in which three traditional carol tunes are mingled and interwoven with an orchestral accompaniment — 'The Truth from Above', the 'Sussex' carol, and 'Come all ye worthy gentlemen — '. A 'cello obbligato reminds the ear that this music is by the author of the 'Tallis' Fantasia, but it is a small and faintly disappointing work, and did not meet our larger need. For myself, I have been secretly willing Vaughan Williams to write a big Christmas Oratorio ever since I discovered his music.

That Fantasia was inextricably, by its well-known themes, wedded to the Christmas season. What is the mysterious quality that makes a carol sound like Christmas? To the ordinary listener this is one of the mysteries of music. It is just possible to understand how even an amateur can know at once the nationality of a folk-tune; how it can be impossible to confuse a French one with a German, or either with one from England or Scotland. But how is it that the Christmas season imposes its special quality on a melody so that the amateur can instantly say of a tune — 'Undoubtedly French, but also a carol'? This Christmas quality is recaptured also in modern carol tunes. Vaughan Williams's 'Wither's Rocking Hymn'; Rubbra's 'Dormi Jesu' and Holst's 'In the bleak midwinter' could never be mistaken for tunes that could be sung at any time of the year. 'Hodie', like the 'Messiah', is different. It is more universal. Only in rare moments has it that sweet haunting quality of Christmas.

Therefore there was no incongruity in hearing the bright splendour of this work in Worcester in September and hardly any Christmas atmosphere crept about the arches of the Cathedral. The music was universal praise for an event attached to no season, to be celebrated any day and every day of the year. The two unaccompanied chorales have, indeed, this Christmas magic, but they are small and lovely localised moments in a work that is long and covers many atmospheres. This is one of Vaughan Williams's 'anthology' works — a compiling of a continuous narrative of the Christmas story from diverse sources, an illustration of each episode by a different example of his musical style.

There was a tinge of dissatisfaction in the notices that followed that first performance, which the composer had himself conducted, and the complaints took a not unfamiliar form —

'Vaughan Williams has said nothing new.' Perhaps there was some truth in them, but Worcester Cathedral swallowed up a good deal of the bright glory among its arches, glory that was starkly revealed in all its harshness in the Festival Hall in the following January. No such dissatisfaction was felt by the choir, who were going about the Cathedral and the city for weeks before, declaring their joy in this new big work. But their enthusiasm must, I suppose, be discounted. Vaughan Williams's music is always glorious to sing, and, as a conductor, he knows very well how to keep his choir happy. If there is nothing new in this cantata (the word seems too small, but there it is on the score) that is only right in a work designed to fill this Christmas gap, to be instantly appreciated by the most ordinary listener. An 'avant garde' and difficult Christmas cantata is surely the last thing that even a critic wants to hear.

The work is dedicated to Herbert Howells, a composer whose music shows the influence of Vaughan Williams's style; whose 'Missa Sabrinensis', a work altogether more sophisticated than 'Hodie', had been performed the day before. Vaughan Williams, in a note in the score, acknowledges his debt to another earlier Three Choirs work of Howells's — 'Dear Herbert, I find that in this cantata I have inadvertently cribbed a phrase from your beautiful "Hymnus Paradisi". Your passage seems so germane to my context that I have decided to keep it.'

The score is for a large orchestra with a big percussion section, and includes bells, a celesta, a glockenspiel and a piano as well as the organ. There are three soloists, soprano, tenor, baritone; a chorus; and a separate semi-chorus of boys' voices who sing in a unison plainsong fashion a linking narration taken from the gospels, between each separate vocal or choral item. They have their own special characteristic accompaniment on the organ alone, making a sweet, gentle and rather Catholic sound against the Protestant vigour of the rest of the music. Vaughan Williams has gleaned widely for his texts — the Vespers for Christmas Day; Milton's Ode on the Morning of Christ's Nativity; Coverdale ; Hardy ; Herbert; Drummond of Hawthornden. There exist practically no Epiphany poems in the English language, so he was fortunate in having the collaboration of Ursula Wood, his wife, who supplied the deficiency with an admirable and suitable poem.

The jubilation of the prologue is heralded by a splendid fanfare on the brass, like a trump from the heavens. The chorus hurl themselves into the music with cries of 'Nowell! Nowell!' rising to a fortissimo climax. Men's voices in unison announce the good news — 'Hodie, Hodie, Christus natus est — '. A note in the score reads 'the English may be sung at the discretion of the conductor, but the composer would much prefer the Latin', a plea one can hardly imagine a conductor would resist. It is said that the composer much prefers the Latin title to the alternative 'This Day', but he does not invariably have his own way over this in the performances so far given. The entire chorus now take up the words of the Latin vespers rising, progressively more joyous, to a succession of 'Glorias' in swaying chords. Then joy seems to overflow all bounds and the 'Glorias' stream downwards in counterpoint as if from the host of heaven. 'Alleluia' answers the earth, marching upwards to meet the angels. The universe appears positively drunk with joy and unites in a joyful dance rhythm that, in a Cathedral, is very nearly too gay to sound quite proper. The movement ends with further jubilant cries of 'Nowell!' while the orchestra blow, bang and scrape their own rejoicing in support of the chorus.

The first narration, like most of the succeeding ones, is introduced, after a pause, by a gentle little twist of notes on the organ, sweet, feminine and remote after the great noise. The children's voices tell how 'the birth of Jesus Christ was on this wise — ', grave and simple and perfectly unemotional. But when they reach the account of Joseph's dream a tissue of mysterious sound echoes out of the orchestra; strings vibrate, the harp is struck, the air tingles; the brass carries a menace of awe. A descending phrase of five notes, twice repeated on the wind, carries us right back to 'Job'. Here, not identical with the phrase in that work, but like enough to be unmistakable, is the gracious, majestic, irresistible voice of God — the voice first heard in 'Sancta Civitas', making once more His intervention in human affairs. A deliberate quotation or a simple unconscious association of ideas? — it does not matter which. It is intensely moving, especially at the first hearing. Then the angel, the tenor voice, singing over an awesome accompaniment of vibrating chords, repeats his message to Joseph with melismatic phrases that repeat the pattern of the voice from heaven. The chorus, with tender majesty, rise to add their prophecy — 'He shall be great, and shall be called the Son of the Highest. Emmanuel; Emmanuel; God with us.'

After the formality and the majesty, Milton's hymn, 'It was the winter wild — ', breaks the tension with its gentle triple-rhythmed flow. The soprano sings the lovely lilting melody, two verses by herself, joined later by the women of the chorus who repeat a rocking refrain heard at the beginning in the orchestra, first singing wordlessly, and then joining in the hymn. The lulling character of the music is suggested better by the words of the third verse than by the first — 'But peaceful was the night — ', for there is no wildness and hardly any winter in this easeful rhythm. Christmas is not localised here, there is no snow and no yule logs; where, at other points in the score, it is given a local flavour, it is one of oriental splendour, not of English ice and winter.

The following narration is plain story-telling, uninterrupted by any dramatic episodes, reaching this time to the actual birth of Christ. 'And she laid him in a manger because there was no room for them in the inn.'

What follows is a quiet, slow, unaccompanied chorale:

> *The blessed son of God only*
> *In a crib full poor did lie;*

humble, gentle, unassuming and as plain as music can be, it is the most completely anonymous tune Vaughan Williams ever composed, without a turn of phrase to give his identity away. Not one accidental intrudes and the harmony is of the simplest hymn-book kind. At a first hearing it seems almost too humbly ordinary, at a longer acquaintance it reveals itself as the most precious jewel in the setting of this splendid cantata. Time stands still and one listens to it with the breath held.

The boys' narration carries us on to the shepherds and their visitation by the angel hosts, so that again the trebles' plainsong leads to the mysterious tremolando of the Angel Gabriel's accompaniment, the moving reminiscence of God's intervention, and a solo passage from the soprano introducing the chorus who, as the heavenly host, sing again 'Glory to God in the highest'. This is followed by another choral passage, not this time drunken, but reverent in its joy, in which the Communion service words 'we praise Thee, we bless Thee, we worship Thee, we magnify Thee' are sung in counterpoint by the men to the 'Glory to Thee' of the women. This timeless union of simplicity with glory, of tenderness with majesty, as in the heavenly dances from 'Job', is surely Vaughan Williams's unique contribution to music and to religion — an attitude of mind not even to be found in the music of Bach. The boys end the chorus, singing in unison — 'and they came with haste and found Mary, and Joseph, and the babe lying in the manger — '.

This perfectly straightforward telling of the Christmas story is interrupted now by Hardy's poem, 'The Oxen,' a modern, half-nostalgic looking-back to past faith and the events of the first Christmas Day. It is strange, detached and revealing — showing how, as with the near quotation from 'Job', certain ideas, styles, associations will call up always a similar response. For this song, for baritone solo and orchestra, is so exactly the music of the early Housman days that at one point it is hard not to feel it must have been written simultaneously with 'On Wenlock Edge'. The thinner, oddly bitter-sweet music of the days before two wars is exactly recalled in the astringent woodwind calls of the introduction, and when the baritone cries — 'Come, see the oxen kneel!' his might be the same voice that cries 'Come all to church, good people — ' in the song 'Bredon Hill'. It calls one back not to Christmas but to the spring of the century. I was not born till after 'Bredon Hill' had been composed, but because I know and love the atmosphere of those early songs, 'The Oxen' affects me with a nostalgia as sharp and piercing as if I had in fact lived in 1909 when Vaughan Williams was writing this sort of music.

'And the shepherds returned, glorifying and praising God —' the trebles continue, and, once again, but this time pianissimo, tranquillo and remote (the chorus remain sitting), the heavenly strains are repeated, 'Glory to God in the highest.'

The baritone has yet another song, a tranquil 'Pastoral' to the poem by Herbert, 'The Shepherds sing, and shall I silent be, my God, no hymn for thee?', floating his melody over an uninterrupted, running triple accompaniment from the orchestra. 'But Mary kept all these things, and pondered them in her heart' sing the trebles, leading to yet another lullaby, for women's voices only, with the familiar words 'Sweet was the song the Virgin sang'. The chorus set the lulling rhythm, and the soprano's voice soars over them with 'Lulla, Lulla, Lullaby'. This is another of those tunes, written throughout Vaughan Williams's life, in which he so fits his melody around the words that one hearing is enough to fix it in the mind forever, as if the tune had always existed, implied in the contour of the poet's words.

The tenor's hymn, by Drummond of Hawthornden, is songwriting of the opposite kind. It is a quite unexpected setting of words that do not in themselves seem to imply music, and the singer's notes do not fix themselves in the mind. It is rather the accompaniment one remembers. The ancient, rather strange words call forth Vaughan Williams's newest music — hard and glittering like the syllables of the poem:

> Bright portals of the sky,
> Emboss'd with sparkling stars,
> Doors of eternity,
> With diamantine bars,
> Your arras rich uphold,
> Loose all your bolts and springs,
> Ope wide your leaves of gold,
> That in your roofs may come the King of Kings.

The little trumpet-fanfare introduction, the celesta, the shimmering strings, the direction 'allegro maestoso', make up a faceted, shining, crystalline picture — hard glittering sound in which the melody is nothing, the effect of icy ecstasy everything. The air is vibrant with the prismatic colour of the 'Antartica's' descriptive passages.

The organ gives a longer introduction to the succeeding narration, solemnly preparing for the slow pageantry of Epiphany; the approaching procession of the Three Kings from afar off. Alone for the first time, the orchestra announces a march — coming from a distance, growing, barbaric, touched with points of gold from the cymbal clashes, rising in excitement. Remembering the march in 'Flos Campi', it is tempting to call this sort of music 'Vaughan Williams oriental'. Enjoyable, compelling to the senses over its plucked and marching bass — a device that Vaughan Williams does not seem to have used for a long time — perhaps a little vulgar; it was the episode picked out by those who do not like Vaughan Williams's music or who wished to suggest that at eighty-one he was beginning to fail in originality, to discredit the whole work. It was also the episode most enjoyed by listeners unfamiliar with his idiom, because here was music that anybody could enjoy at a first hearing.

The tenors and basses in unison join in the march theme and the words of Ursula Wood's poem:

> From kingdoms of wisdom secret and far
> come Caspar, Melchior, Balthasar;
> they ride through time, they ride through night,
> led by the star's foretelling light.

The women add their voices for the climax of the Kings' arrival at the stable of the Nativity. Three verses, telling each of one of the three gifts, are given to the soloists — gold to the baritone; frankincense to the tenor, mysteriously accompanied; myrrh, 'a bitter gift for the dead', to the soprano. The passage is softly concluded by the chorus — 'Your way is short, your days foretold.' A cymbal roll reintroduces the march tune, fortissimo, and the Kings are adjured to return to their 'Kingdoms secret and far'. The oriental and splendid music dies away into the distance with a long diminuendo.

Immediately the chorus begin their second unaccompanied chorale, another lullaby, entirely different from the first chorale with its plain familiar harmonies — 'No sad thoughts his soul affright' — strange, cold, yet tender, hushing, 'sempre pianissimo,' alternating between minor and major, with an astringent, almost eerie effect. Again here, as in the first chorale, with the orchestra silent, time seems to stand still in a patch of absolute awe and breathlessness.

The epilogue is solemn at its opening, with a succession of chords in pairs that seem to come out of 'The Pilgrim's Progress' and the Symphony in D. The three soloists, taking each a sentence, sing the most solemn and formal passage from the gospels — 'In the beginning was the Word, and the Word was with God, and the Word was God.' The majestic angel's phrase is repeated, and all the chorus unite again to repeat their declaration — 'Emmanuel, Emmanuel, God with us', out of the prologue. And once again joy is released. The whole chorus leap into the last three verses of Milton's hymn *On the Morning of Christ's Nativity* — 'Ring out, ye crystal spheres' — , assisted by organ, bells, glockenspiel, piano and every instrument in the orchestra that can add bite and colour. It is a terrestrial rejoicing, not heavenly like the opening chorus, not drunk with joy nor mazed with wonder, but earthy and satisfied — man stamping with his heavy boots upon the solid world. This is the point at which one dearly wishes all the audience could leap to their feet and add their voices to the universal song. Perhaps, a century from now, this work that so fulfils our Christmas need may have become so familiar that that might happen automatically. Now there is nothing we can do but applaud enthusiastically — a thing not possible when this work is heard in church. Perhaps the lack of applause accounts for the slight feeling of flatness that followed the first performance in Worcester Cathedral. For Vaughan Williams does none of the things that one expects of him at the end of this work, there is no distant soprano to have the last word, and no soft fading down to his usual 'niente'. He does the obvious — builds to his climax, brings in every resource he has in a tremendous explosion of delight, and breaks off cleanly at the peak with a loud shout.

This loud shout, I had expected and intended, was going to be, for me, the end and climax of this book. The book had to end somewhere, however great might be the temptation to wait a little longer to see what new territory Vaughan Williams would be found exploring next. In the autumn of 1955 the existence of an eighth symphony was revealed and a date announced for its performance by the Hallé Orchestra in Manchester. It proved, in its final movement, to be the loudest shout of all.

The Symphony in D minor is dedicated to Sir John Barbirolli, who, with the Hallé Orchestra, had given the first performance of the immediately preceding symphony, the 'Sinfonia Antartica'. There could be no dedication more appropriate. No orchestra could have been better chosen to perform this fresh and glittering music, in which every instrument, every section, is given its chance to show its paces in separate themes and in whole movements. That the Hallé enjoyed it mightily was reflected equally in their expressions of delight (especially a fierce dedicated joy on the faces of the five percussion players who are required by the score) and in the incomparable precision of their playing. Here, even more than in the 'Antartica', is a work in which this team of musicians can shine their brightest. The music, without a hint or a shadow of a programme or a moral or a message, turns over and over in delight; now sensuous, now witty, finally blatantly cacophonous; reserving its profoundest meditation for a dark slow movement for the strings alone.

The composer's irreverent programme notes — notes that have been growing more delightfully wicked with every work since the Symphony in E minor — gave everybody some excuse for wondering if the new work was a symphony at all. In his notes for the D minor he does not actually refer to his usual enemy 'the official analyst', but the following paragraph is plainly directed at this sinister shadowy personage. It has already been quoted many times, and will continue to be quoted, because it is a delight in

itself, and because it is not only witty but exact. 'I understand that
some hearers may have their withers wrung by a work being called
a symphony whose first movement does not correspond to the
usual symphonic form. It may perhaps be suggested that by a little
verbal jugglery this movement may be referred to the conventional scheme. Thus, the first section may be called the first subject; the second (presto) section can become the 'bridge passage';
the third section, starting at (d), may be described as the second
subject. Sections four and five we will call the development, the
allegro will be the reprise of the first subject, though this, I admit,
will be skating over rather thin ice: but there will be no difficulty
in referring the final section to the recapitulation and coda. Thus
all wounds will be healed and honour satisfied.'

Doubts about the symphony's status among the eight, however,
do not come from the unusual form of the first movement, which
is wonderfully satisfying, no matter from which angle you choose
to look at it. Judging it not so much from experience of other
people's symphonies as from familiarity with Vaughan Williams's
own, it does seem to stand a little apart from the rest. It is not so
much that it is lighter, but that it does not seem to have that
tremendous drive straight through the movements that carries the
listener on from the first note to the last of, at any rate, the central
four symphonies, the 'Pastoral'; the F minor (most closely-knit of
all Vaughan Williams's works); the D major with its surface
tranquillity and its underlying solidity; the E minor whose shape
is unconventional and utterly convincing. Not even in the 'Sinfonia Antartica' can one imagine the possibility of arresting the
music's progress in midstream to repeat a movement. But it would
not seem incongruous or even particularly immoral to isolate the
Scherzo or the Cavatina of the D minor Symphony and play them,
for their own sake, alone. The shape of the symphony is logical
and pleasing — a general movement for the entire orchestra; a
Scherzo for the wind; a Cavatina for strings; and a final paean of a
Toccata in which 'all the available hitting instruments which can
make definite notes' do their best to drown the rest of the orchestra and burst the eardrums of the audience. Each successive hear-

ing reveals this symphony as more of an integrated whole. It is a question of accustoming oneself to a symphony by Vaughan Williams that does not lean towards a weighty last movement. His familiar epilogue is missing.

'This music has no meaning', the composer was heard to say, in possible exasperation at meanings persistently read into earlier symphonies. This time he seems to have had his way and I have not heard a word of attempted interpretation from any side. Nobody, surely, could dream of reading meanings into this music, which is golden and happy for three of its movements, with just one to stir the heart to immortal longings. There is only the one meaning that has always lain behind every note Vaughan Williams has set down on paper — to see 'the glimpses of the heart of things' and to crystallise them for us into 'earthly sound'.

The symphony is scored for what the composer chooses to call 'the "Schubert" orchestra; with the addition of a harp'. In fact two harps appear, though it is permissible to omit one. It certainly does not look like a 'Schubert' orchestra assembled on the platform, and this is principally due to the five players standing possessively over their 'large supply of extra percussion, including all the 'phones and 'spiels known to the composer'. Besides the usual timpani the onlooker can locate a side drum, triangle, tubular bells, cymbals, bass drum, xylophone, glockenspiel, celesta, tunable gongs 'as used by Puccini in "Turandot"', and, of course, Vaughan Williams's new, and not altogether respectable, love, the vibraphone. 'The gongs,' says the composer, 'are not absolutely essential but highly desirable.' He uses them to make a noise that is louder than anything in 'Turandot' and as unlike Puccini as any music he has ever written. The symphony suffers a little, at first hearing, from being much too interesting to look at, and it is possible to forget the music altogether in a desire not to miss the lady (it was a lady in the Hallé Orchestra) performing glissandi on the bells with both hands at once.

It is out of three little figures, a four-note trumpet call leading to some chords on the vibraphone (a); a melody for the flute of a distinctly Indian flavour (*b*); and a few descending notes on the violins (*c*) that the seven Variazioni Senza Tema grow. The movement, the composer tells us, 'has been nicknamed "seven variations in search of a theme" '. (*a*) begins with a quiet trumpet call which is a pair of rising fourths. It is like a signature. 'Here', says the trumpet in four notes, 'is a work by Vaughan Williams.' 'Yes indeed,' replies the vibraphone, with five chords, 'and you can tell by my voice that it is a recent one.' The critic of the *Manchester Guardian* complained that the vibraphone had gone to Vaughan Williams's head. Under the influence of this music it seems to have gone to my head too, and I could have welcomed even more of the glimmering soft atmosphere of this first variation — as ravishing and strange an opening as a symphony ever had. Before the London performance Vaughan Williams suppressed some of the percussion in the last movement, which had called forth some horribly disapproving comments from the press. About the vibraphone he remained properly unrepentant. So far from suppressing it, he countered critical comment in a short broadcast introduction to the symphony which he made for overseas, by referring to it, with, I am sure, a glint of battle in his eye, as 'the beautiful, comparatively modern vibraphone'. I think perhaps that he has said now all that he needs to say with this distinctive instrument, but I am unrepentant also in finding it, in the context of this first movement of the D minor Symphony, entirely beautiful and right. This first variation, with its trumpet call, echoed by the horn, and the bassoon and harp; its vibraphone and celesta decorations; and its oriental flute theme, seems bent on transporting the listener to some place of Arabian Nights' fantasy, with a sensuality of sounds more luxurious than anything to be found in 'Flos Campi' or the minuet from 'Job'. 'Voluptuous' was the composer's direction for that dance. I think it is the word for the beginning of this symphony. In the second variation '(*a*), (*b*) and (*c*) are juggled about by wind and strings'. This is a hurrying twilit 'presto' that whisks one away from the soft enchantment to some place between the 'Pastoral's' headlong coda and the macabre Scherzo of the Symphony in D. It becomes clear that the

fourths that now scamper upwards are going to come into opposi-
tion with (c), the descending figure for strings, which presently
appears firmly and rather crossly striding down on the wind and
the violins. The third variation breaks, after a silence, on an off-
beat, almost hesitantly, on the strings and harp. 'Andante soste-
nuto', 'a choral-like melody appears . . . which proves to be a
descant of (a). This leads to a cantabile phrase for oboe and solo
violoncello which seems to be another variation of (a).' 'Proves to
be', 'seems to be', thus always does Vaughan Williams write about
his music, as if he were not quite responsible for the direction in
which his three little 'isolated figures' were going to lead him.
The choral is played on the higher strings, while the lower ones
repeat the rising fourths to which it 'proves' the descant. Then the
oboe and a solo 'cello begin their transformation of (a), decorat-
ing, softening and drawing it out into those long threads of undulating melody that are familiar to us even from the early songs.
Flute, oboe, horns, a solo clarinet, then all the woodwind play
with it over chords from the harps. The strings repeat a little of
their comforting choral. Is it the rising fourths, an interval that
characterised every movement of the 'London' Symphony, or is
it those long graceful strains spun by the woodwind that remind
the ear of that early symphony, and, in particular, of the development section of the first movement with its threads of melody
and its golden chain of harp notes? In a sense, I suppose, this can
claim to be another 'Symphony by a Londoner', for, after many
years in the country, Vaughan Williams has returned to live in
London, in one of its greenest places. But the strands of music are
now not quite so English and by Variation 4, an allegretto in six-
eight time that produces yet more variants upon (a), the atmosphere is again curiously oriental. A pair of rising fourths in the
hands of Vaughan Williams seem capable of infinite development,
of producing more solid music in one movement than one might
find in a year of other people's symphonies. The third fragment
plays a part in this variation, infusing it with an atmosphere of
mystery. The fifth variation is aqueous, liquid; an upward expansion of, again, (a), on the harp and 'cellos, producing a watery

sound that has an echo of Alan Rawsthorne. Here, in this lovely limpid movement, in which not a note is wasted or obscured, Vaughan Williams seems again to be experimenting with new sounds and textures, this time soft and glimmering ones as a change from the hard and icy textures he explored in the 'Antartica'. 'A perversion of (*b*)', the flute's tune, and (*a*) in a simpler form make the sixth variation — the 'rather thin ice' or reprise of the first subject of the analysis — and it leads us up to what we hoped and believed would surely follow, 'a repetition on a larger and more grandiose scale of the third section,' that is, of the beautiful choral. But 'grandiose' is not the word at all, though Elgar, with whose music some of the textures in this symphony have been compared, would have made it so. Vaughan Williams cannot be grandiose, any more than he can (except for comic effect) be pompous. The drawn-out climax, largamente, of this wonderful tune gives another example of his astonishing skill in building up a movement; like the first of the D major Symphony, the last of the 'Pastoral'. It is as if, expecting yet another climb before us, we found that he had led us round a corner to what proved to be the summit of the range, and presented us with a complete and magnificent view, vaster and more expansive than anything that, in the beginning, he had promised to show. The conversation by the way, the sights to be admired, have been so various and diverting that we had no notion that we had, in fact, arrived, or that, when we did arrive, the reward would be of this nature. The downward steps of the choral tune help to return us safely to the ground whence we started out, and we are back with the flute and the bassoon singing their Indian theme, the trumpet with its rising fourths, the vibraphone, the celesta. The movement ends on a long-held chord on the violins.

I believe that Vaughan Williams takes a delight in lulling his audiences into a condition of relaxed dreaming and then waking us briskly by the musical equivalent of pouring a bucket of water over our heads. Twice in this symphony of contrasts he does this to us. In the brief seconds that separate one movement from the next Caliban's words had come into my mind:

the isle is full of noises,
Sounds and sweet airs that give delight, and hurt not.
Sometimes a thousand twangling instruments
Will hum about mine ears; and sometimes voices,
That, if I then had wak'd after long sleep,
Will make me sleep again, and then, in dreaming,
The clouds methought would open, and show riches
Ready to drop on me, that, when I wak'd,
I cried to dream again,

for this first movement that sways astonishingly between the Indies and Gloucestershire or Regent's Park, has the same blend of improbable fantasy with a tender firmness that *The Tempest* has. Let me not be misunderstood for a single moment in making this comparison between Vaughan Williams's Eighth Symphony and Shakespeare's last play. The composer's admirers are already beginning to speculate on the possible form and character of his Ninth Symphony. Shakespeare chose to retire. A retired Vaughan Williams is inconceivable. The comparison suggests itself because, when seeking to describe this music, 'golden' is the adjective that keeps coming into my mind, as it would if I were describing the quality of that play.

The Scherzo whips us firmly out of the dream. What a pity it was that Ravel could not have been present in the Free Trade Hall on the first night of the symphony! Maybe, as one critic suggested, it was as well that he could not hear those bells in the last movement. It is the second that I would wish him to have heard. Might he not have learnt a thing or two himself from this neat little Scherzo alla Marcia composed by the pupil who went to him because he believed himself to be 'lumpy and stodgy'? Never has the 'French polish' which Vaughan Williams went to Paris to acquire shone so brightly. (Perhaps French is not quite what it sounds.) Some composers have been severely reprimanded by their government for writing music very like this. It is only another paradox among many that not one phrase of this elegant and funny little piece could have been put together by any other composer in the world, and yet the total effect is entirely untypical.

N

Vaughan Williams has always had a deft hand with a Scherzo, but in this one his rhythms are squarer, there is not the usual cross-rhythmic interest; it is completely and delightfully prosaic, almost a little prim. What a useful weapon a recording of this Scherzo will be to refute accusations from the people who still persist in considering his music 'lumpy and stodgy'! The bassoons are the protagonists with a tune that runs and jumps among airily-spaced staccato chords. The trumpet follows with a tune that is as Cockney as anything in the 'London' Symphony; a little, politer, 'oompah' drops in to accompany it from the F minor. After all this strict-time breeziness, this efficient blowing (one feels that the brass will give an extra polish to their instruments before setting out on this Scherzo) there is a neat section of fugal writing 'which is started by the bassoons and carried on with various devices, such as stretto, augmentation, etc., by the rest of the band'. The depressed little trio is in six-eight time for contrast and is another perfectly Indian tune strayed on to the wrong instruments. It is like a ghostly parody of all the composer's earlier, heavier trios. This sad little band droops to its finish and immediately the brisk efficiency of the squarer rhythm of the opening is resumed. It does not linger. It is, as the composer tells us, a 'truncated recapitulation' — 'a short stretto and a few bars of coda'. The movement ends deliciously with a tiny flourish, and cannot fail to make its audience laugh out loud.

The principal theme of the slow movement, a Cavatina for the strings alone, is a cantilena twelve bars long, heard first on the violoncellos, while the basses pluck an occasional note below and the strings higher in the register begin to draw threads of sound above. The tone is impersonal, remote; the effect more like the sound of a string quartet than of a full orchestra. There is about the opening of this music a desolation, a loneliness like the bleak but beautiful Epilogue of the E minor Symphony, perhaps through relationship of key. A 'short episode of which we shall hear more later' mentioned in the composer's notes, descending on the violins after the 'cellos have finished their long tune, is cold also. When the violins claim the 'cellos' theme their sound is still impersonal and passionless, but the little scales that the 'cellos and basses interject, running upwards, pizzicato, questioning, begin to have a hint of warmth and ardour. Then, out of a silence, and again, as with the choral of the first movement, with an odd hesitation, we hear 'an important second section in triple time'. In this way, I suppose, with cold detachment, it is proper for composers to describe their perfect inventions. The melody is uttered, heavily, on all the strings in solid harmony; a melody that seems at first to bring warmth and peace and comfort against the uncoloured disembodied first part of the movement; but the peace vanishes before the end into infinite longing and despair, even as the cor anglais theme from the Romanza of the D major Symphony ended. The development section, founded on a figure that relates to the first bar of the 'cellos' tune, employs something of the methods used in the 'Tallis' Fantasia of reaching a climax of almost equally unbearable tenseness, without achieving anything like the ecclesiastical richness of that string music. Again Vaughan Williams cannot forbear to introduce an old friend; his solo violin, in a 'cadenza-like passage', makes his voice heard once more, first 'appassionata' over an accompaniment, and again, when the climax has been achieved, in perfect loneliness. The restatement of the first theme is expanded by the addition of the violas and basses while the violins interrupt with a sad little downward figure. The wonderful second tune is repeated in a shortened version. The movement, which throughout has swung between a cold remoteness and a warm passionate tone that is, none the less, uncoloured by a hint of romance, ends warmly with a solo 'cello playing, up from its very depths, a cadenza founded on the violin's figure that opened the development. Why do we try to imprison music in words? In the two principal Sunday papers, the week-end after the symphony's first performance, there were notices. One said of this movement that it was 'tinged with the melancholy of a man gazing on beauty less transient than himself'; the other that the movement had 'no hint of sadness'. Perhaps music of this thoughtful, philosophic kind depends partly on what the listener brings to it. I found that it grew slowly on me, seeming at first hearing a little remote. Like the 'Tallis' Fantasia it deepens at every hearing. Vaughan Williams has written music like this before, and I can see no reason why he should not write music like it again, and again, as often as he feels he wants to. This is a movement that will last me a lifetime.

After the divine discontent of this Cavatina, added to the delicious fun of the Scherzo, and the inexhaustible richness of the Variations, who am I to be superior if Vaughan Williams wishes to finish his symphony in a burst of rude high spirits that shatters our mood of meditation? I would not deny him a single gong or 'phone or 'spiel to hit in his Toccata, though I must admit that I would not be sorry if he mislaid the tubular bells, which always sound flat to me, until the glorious moment when the famous glissandi are performed on them — a noise which I would not have him cut for all the world. I only wish that I had a 'phone or 'spiel of my own to offer him to add to his battery of noises. I can only direct his attention to an orchestra that came over here a few years ago to accompany some dancers from Bali. It was principally composed of tunable percussion, and I am sure it would give him much to think about. What would Holst have had to say about this movement; Holst who almost went down on his knees to beg Vaughan Williams to cut out half of the percussion in the relatively sober score of 'Job'? Between Manchester and London some of the percussion was cut, and the movement seemed no less triumphant in sound for its slight pruning. I cannot find it in me to disapprove or find unsuitable the loud and mood-shattering finale of this work; the whole of the symphony is unconventional in scheme, and there were enough 'unsymphonic' noises in the first movement to prepare one for anything at all. Vaughan Williams has said, 'I could not put down on paper a note that I did not feel in every part of me,' and this we cannot doubt to be the literal truth. Then what can we do but envy one who feels this exuberance, this joy, this compelling urge to 'make a joyful noise unto the God of Jacob', no matter what frowns, what critical raised eyebrows the noises may provoke? This 'modified rondo' turns out to be in its own right, and by association of themes with other works, a 'Benedicite' of bells and gongs; an extension to the xylophone, the vibraphone, the celesta, of 'Let all the world in every corner sing, My God and King!'; a further jubilation for the Sons of the Morning to the accompaniment of those glissandi on the bells. Nobody but the composer seems to have been able to detect anything 'sinister' in the 'exordium', which is also the end of the symphony. The mood of the movement is pure exultation, and if not very refined or exquisite or civilised, perhaps that is the composer reminding us that we do not, in fact, expect, or particularly desire, him to be any of these things — and making up for having been them all to an unusual extent in his first three movements. Though he can no longer, after that Scherzo, ever dare to claim the title 'amateur' again, he does his best to show himself unchanged; unteachable, incorrigible, and gloriously unrepentant. I do hope that the gentleman who, on the day before the first performance, described him as an 'aloof and seer-like figure in whose presence lesser men and women spoke in lower tones' was there to hear that noise, and the riot of applause and shouting that followed it.

Vaughan Williams's Symphony in D minor, in spite of the shocked tone of some of its notices, is already a success. Whether it deserves its success as much as some of its predecessors is something that nobody can tell for a long time; but if it does not, that is not because it is light or gay or golden, which are qualities that are surely as precious in a symphony as in any music. The composer himself received as great and moving an ovation, both in Manchester and in London, as he has ever had in all his seventy-seven years of composing. At each of the three performances the audience rose spontaneously to their feet in pure affection and respect to applaud him till our hands were sore with clapping; while he, exactly recalling his programme notes, made little gestures as if to disclaim all responsibility for the music, as if the orchestra had, without any assistance from him, conjured it out of the air. This ovation, this demonstration of possessive love for our most honoured composer, happened to come at the end of each performance of the Symphony in D minor. I think he could

R.V.W.

have had it for the asking at any time in the last ten years or more, for all our traditional musical apathy. But in all but one of his other symphonies he has forbidden, made impossible, any such demonstration, by determinedly ending his last movement pianissimo, niente. In the D minor it is, at last, no vulgarity to leap to one's feet, almost before the last note has died away, and add to the percussion.

These paragraphs had to be written during and immediately after the fortnight which heard the two Manchester performances of this new symphony and the one in London, while I was still caught in the golden glitter of its uniquely translucent airy improbability — for this is the most improbable symphony Vaughan Williams has ever given us — and in the warm, contagious glow of those loving receptions. A music critic can go straight away and telephone his paper, or write a cold and accurate analysis of the work he has heard. He can put it in its place. I cannot. I, like the average ordinary listener, have no idea what place in my affections the Symphony in D minor will ultimately occupy. It will be months, perhaps years, before I am sure, though I am already certain that I will never be able to stay away from a single performance of it. Notes like these should not be written in an atmosphere of intoxication. As I went into the Festival Hall for the London performance — the last foreseeable one for the moment — my exhilaration had calmed temporarily into a slight sadness. I had these notes to finish and send off to the printer, the last notes that can come into the compass of this book, although Vaughan Williams has, inevitably, beaten me to the post with yet another new work — 'A Vision of Aeroplanes' — to be given its first performance less than five weeks after the new symphony. I was torn between happy anticipation of the symphony's first London performance, and London's reception of it, and the knowledge that when I left the hall I would feel flat and lost and sad. Then I was brought to a standstill by the sight of a poster. There it was — Symphony No. 4 in F minor. Vaughan Williams —about three weeks ahead. Of course I had not come to an end. I was back again where I had started. I went straight off and bought a ticket.

EPILOGUE

I started writing these chapters partly to try to pass on to other ordinary listeners like myself some of the joy I discovered when I found out the existence of the music of Vaughan Williams. But I think I wrote them principally to try to discover for myself what mysterious ingredient in his music made him, for me, the most worthwhile composer that all the ages had to offer — a composer so satisfying to my mind that I would not be too distressed if I had to spend the rest of my life with his music and his alone. I cannot say that I am much nearer the answer. I am only more convinced than when I began that my bones are not far wrong when they cry out that Vaughan Williams is not only one of the most considerable of living composers, but one of the most astonishing that have ever lived; one that has reached, perhaps, further out on all sides towards the boundaries of human experience, thought and knowledge than any other, of any day and age. But that, if it is a fact, is no explanation. For every one of us there exist great composers who, admire them as we may, fail to stir one muscle of our scalp or raise one shiver of our spine. Perhaps it is necessary for me that my composer should be as easily capable of throwing together that shatteringly blatant collection of tunes that makes up the rowdy finale to 'The Wasps' Suite as of composing the remote and icy Sanctus of the Mass in G minor; of belabouring my ears with the Protestant percussiveness of the 'Benedicite' in one concert and wooing them with the near-saccharine sweetness of the 'Serenade to Music' in the next; of composing the heavenly enigma of 'Flos Campi' which, I have heard said, breaks every known rule of harmony on its first page, and enlivening our Church services with his plain and diatonic hymns; of turning from the harsh discordant horror of Job's nightmares to the golden notes of Elihu's enchanted violin and through them to the Sons of the Morning with their rollicking sea-shanty of a tune that is none the less the very breath of heaven. Perhaps it is necessary for me that my composer should be impolite, wilfully clumsy on occasion, 'content to provide good plain cooking', taking no trouble at all to cultivate the art that conceals art. Perhaps I could solve the problem quite simply by saying that I, like my favourite composer, have a 'Leidenschaft' for the flattened seventh. But most probably it is partly because Vaughan Williams himself prepared the way for me, by his labours, alongside some of his contemporaries, to create in England a state of affairs in which music could once more flourish; labours so extensive that one wonders sometimes how he was able to find time to be a prolific composer as well. But I think that he has given the explanation himself. He wrote it as long ago as 1912 in an article called 'Who wants the English Composer?' 'Is it not possible', he asked, 'that he has something to say to his own countrymen that no one of any other age or country can say? When English people realise this — that the composer is their own voice speaking through his art those things which they can only dimly grope for — then indeed the English composer will be wanted.' Is that not the explanation for that overwhelming sense of recognition, of having at last found something I had been looking for all my life, that overcame me in 1942 listening to that Symphony in F minor? Is it not the explanation for the more astonishing fact that the next work of his that I heard — the 'London' Symphony, so different in technique, in atmosphere, in personality — was completely unsurprising too; that I inferred from that shattering fourth symphony the existence of the sweet and sober third? The eight symphonies are eight separate worlds of his creating — each with its own atmosphere and colour, its own set of rules applicable to no other musical work, its own inner logic. 'It is the essence of modern music,' he wrote, 'as of all modern thought, to drive straight to the root of the matter in hand without artifice or subterfuge; to let the matter rule the form, not the form the matter; to obtain our rules from the practice, not our practice from the rules', and though he was writing as early as 1920, before the 'Pastoral' Symphony, and writing not of his own work but of the music of Gustav Holst, those words

most perfectly describe the means by which those eight symphonies were brought to birth. Through each of them, and
through his other works, this great composer, his mind wide open to
embrace whatever of art, of life, of other music the centuries have
to offer, yet none the less determined at all costs to be himself,
enables us to see 'the glimpses of the heart of things' which he has
'crystallised into earthly sound' for us. Yet always he is at hand to
bring us down to earth again with a common-sense programme
note 'whose chief intent (says *Grove*) seems to be to avoid giving
his hearers a cut-and-dried interpretation of his musical thought',
or with a frank admission of the difficulty overcome, the help
received, before the work was ready for our hearing.

The most joyful fact about any record of Vaughan Williams's
first eighty years is that it is incomplete. Eagerly, as always, we
look forward to his next projected work, grown too wise by this
time to risk any guesses as to its nature; but confident that in it he
will say something he has never said before and that he will have
'taken the trouble to make sure that this was the right thing to say
at the right moment'.

But in this history of my own adventures with his music there
is another incompleteness which I must deplore, for not all my
searching in the past fourteen years has enabled me to catch up
with all Vaughan Williams's long list of compositions. Besides
the Piano Concerto there are other works that are rarely heard
— those strange cold Chaucer Rondels — 'Merciless Beautee';
the Choral Hymns, to words by Miles Coverdale, mystical
poems whose uncompromising setting predicted the composer's
sudden emergence as a writer of 'modern' music early in the
1930's. Shall we ever see on any stage a professional performance
of 'The Poisoned Kiss', or hear again the string quartet that caused
a friend to tell the young Vaughan Williams that he 'must have
been having tea with Debussy'? Must we embark upon a third
world war to be allowed to sing the stark plain unison songs, with
words by Shelley, that the composer called 'Songs to be Sung in
Time of War'? There is the Rossetti 'Willow Wood', the historic
'Toward the Unknown Region'; the rarely-played 'Partita for

Double String Orchestra' with its movement of 'Homage to
Henry Hall'; the Viola Suite; the thunderous 'Introduction and
Fugue for Two Pianos'; the promise of enjoyment in the future is
almost unending.

When I turned on my wireless to assist my ironing in 1942 I let
more into my room and into my life than the music of Vaughan
Williams. If I had realised what powerful forces I was, in that
instant, unchaining, perhaps I would hurriedly have switched the
knob back to the 'off' position. But even if I had not waited to
hear the name of the composer I doubt if the upheaval Peter Warlock wrote of would have passed me by. The damage had been
done. My whole being had, even in those first crashing bars,
responded to the strange new noise, and, from that moment, I
ceased to be content with the music 'chance occasions had to offer'.
For the music of Vaughan Williams, as I hope I have already
shown, cannot fail to lead its hearers onward and outward. Even
as it raised my spirits it brought my pride low. For in the light of
this new discovery all former prejudices had to be reviewed.
From that day onwards I listened with new ears to the music I had
mildly been enjoying all my life, forced suddenly to recognise the
emptiness of many of my old favourites and, infinitely more painful to the soul, to discover beauty in music I had long dismissed as
too blatant or too simple for my refined taste. The music of
Vaughan Williams led me not only to itself but, delightfully, back
to folk-song, to plainsong, to Tudor music, to the wealth of the
remoter past that the ordinary public's polite concert-going hardly
touches. It taught me to listen to Bach with my heart instead of
with my head; to plunge headlong into the writings of my contemporaries with the confidence that my head would emerge
again above the waters; even (but this was the influence of
Vaughan Williams's writing rather than his music) to share his
unholy delight in the fourth movement of Beethoven's Choral
Symphony — a conversion I cannot quite bring myself to forgive!

For Vaughan Williams music is a moral force, and if it were
possible for that to escape a listener to his music there are his many
writings which state his conviction plain and clear. In my ignor-

ance as an ordinary, and, I liked to imagine, discriminating, concert-goer, this fundamental fact had quite escaped me. If I thought
about it at all I regarded music as (to quote Vaughan Williams
quoting the *Encyclopaedia Britannica*) 'an ornament on the fringe
of life'. In the fourteen years of my quest for his music I have discovered the appalling falsity of that comfortable idea; I have
found out the truth of his surprising statement in the *English
Hymnal* preface, that it requires 'a certain effort to tune oneself to
the moral atmosphere implied by a fine melody'. I have discovered
that the curious popular expression 'facing the music', far from
being, as I had imagined, meaningless, describes, in fact, a vivid
and alarming reality.

This book began as the story of an obsession, but at the moment
I seem to have caught, from the composer I write of, his habit of
turning everything into a sermon. I would prefer to leave the
sermons to him. For all I want to do is to shout aloud, to anybody
who will listen, my delight that I was fortunate enough to be born
into this century and not any other. For who, having discovered
and fallen in love with this music, would not willingly endure the
drabness of present-day life and the menace of the hydrogen bomb
and all the other benefits the twentieth century has to offer, for a
lifetime, and, I devoutly hope, an eternity to follow, of the music
of Ralph Vaughan Williams?

BOOKS BY AND ABOUT VAUGHAN WILLIAMS

R. Vaughan Williams, *Some Thoughts on Beethoven's Choral Symphony*, Oxford University Press.

R. Vaughan Williams, *National Music*, Oxford University Press.

R. Vaughan Williams, *The Making of Music*, Cornell University Press.

R. Vaughan Williams (edited), *The English Hymnal*, Oxford University Press.

R. Vaughan Williams (edited), *Songs of Praise*, Oxford University Press.

Hubert Foss, *Ralph Vaughan Williams: A Study*, Harrap.

Percy Young, *Vaughan Williams*, Dennis Dobson.

A. E. F. Dickinson, *Introduction to the Music of Ralph Vaughan Williams*, Oxford University Press.

Frank Howes, *The Music of Ralph Vaughan Williams*, Oxford University Press.

LIST OF GRAMOPHONE RECORDS

The Symphonies

'Sea' Symphony. (1910)
  Isabel Baillie, John Cameron, London Philharmonic
    Orchestra and Choir, Boult.   LXT2907–8
'London' Symphony. (1914, rev. 1920)
  London Philharmonic Orchestra, Boult.   LXT2693
'Pastoral' Symphony. (1922)
  London Philharmonic Orchestra, Boult.   LXT2787
Symphony No. 4 in F minor. (1935)
  London Philharmonic Orchestra, Boult.   LXT2909
Symphony No. 5 in D. (1943)
  London Philharmonic Orchestra, Boult.   LXT2910
Symphony No. 6 in E minor. (1947)
  London Philharmonic Orchestra, Boult.   LXT2911
  London Symphony Orchestra, Boult.   (H)BPL1001
Sinfonia Antartica. (1953)
  M. Ritchie, Hallé Orchestra, Barbirolli.   (H)ALP1102
  J. Gielgud, M. Ritchie, London Philharmonic
    Orchestra and Choir, Boult.   LXT2912
Symphony No. 8 in D minor. (1956)
  Hallé Orchestra, Barbirolli.   NCT17000
  London Philharmonic Orchestra, Boult.   DECCA

Orchestral Works

Job — A Masque for Dancing. (1930)
  London Philharmonic Orchestra, Boult.   LXT2937
Fantasia on a Theme of Thomas Tallis. (1910)
  Philharmonic Promenade Orchestra, Boult.   NPL905
  Philharmonic, Karajan.   33CX1159
  New Symphony Orchestra, Collins.   LXT2699
  B.B.C. Symphony Orchestra, Sargent.   (H)BLP1019
  Stokowski Symphony Orchestra.   (H)ALP1205
The Wasps — Aristophanic Suite. (1909)
  London Philharmonic Orchestra, Boult.   LXT2907
  London Symphony Orchestra, Weldon.   33SX1019

Old King Cole — Ballet Suite. (1923)
    London Philharmonic Orchestra, Boult.   LW5151
A Norfolk Rhapsody. (1908)
    Philharmonic Promenade Orchestra, Boult.   NPL905
English Folk-Song Suite. (transcribed Jacob)
    Philharmonic Promenade Orchestra, Boult.   NPL905
Greensleeves.
    Philharmonic Promenade Orchestra, Boult.   NPL905

Concerti

'Flos Campi' for Viola, Chorus and Orchestra. (1925)
    Tursi, Concert Hall Symphony Orchestra, Hull.   CPL1151
Violin Concerto in D minor. (Accademico)
    Fuchs, Zimbler String Orchestra.   AXTL1006
Concerto for Oboe and Strings. (1944)
    London Symphony Orchestra, Rothwell, Barbirolli. (H)BLP1078
Concerto for Bass Tuba and Orchestra. (1954)
    London Symphony Orchestra, Catelinet, Barbirolli. (H)BLP1078
The Lark Ascending. (1914)
    Pougnet, London Philharmonic Orchestra, Boult.   PMB1003
Romance for Harmonica, Strings and Piano.
    Larry Adler, Sargent.   33S1023

Choral

Five Tudor Portraits. (1936)
    Rankin, Anderson, Choir, Pittsburg Symphony
        Orchestra.   CTL7047
Song of Thanksgiving. (1945)
    Speaight, London Philharmonic Orchestra, Choir,
        Boult.   PMB1003
Mystical Songs. (The Call; I got me flowers; Easter)
    St Paul's Choir.   33CX1193
O Taste and See.
    St Paul's Choir.   33CX1193
Mass in G minor (1922) for solo quartet and double choir. LXT2794

Vocal

I will give my love an apple; The New Ghost.
    Jennifer Vyvyan, Ernest Lush.   LXT2797

On Wenlock Edge. (1909)
A. Young and Sebastian String Quartet.   RG20
George Maran, Ivor Newton, London String Trio.   LW5233
Seven Songs from 'The Pilgrim's Progress'.
Cameron, Kells, Bartlett, Watson.   RG20
Silence and Music — Song. (1953)
Cambridge University Choir.   33CX1063
Silent Noon.
Kathleen Ferrier, Frederick Stone.   LX3313

Military Band
Folk Song Suite.
Toccata Marziale.
Eastman Symphonic Wind Ensemble.   MLR2001

Instrumental
Sonata for Violin and Piano.
Frederick Grinke and Michael Mullinar.   LXT5143

INDEX

PRINTED IN GREAT BRITAIN BY ROBERT MACLEHOSE AND CO. LTD
THE UNIVERSITY PRESS, GLASGOW